David Dale trained at Sydney University to be a psychologist, but decided he would do less harm to the cause of mental health if he moved into journalism. He has been a political reporter for the *Australian* newspaper; a sub-editor for *General Practitioner* magazine in London; New York correspondent for the *Sydney Morning Herald*; editor of the *Bulletin* magazine; breakfast broadcaster for ABC radio; and columnist on popular culture for the *Australian Financial Review*. Between jobs he has travelled to most corners of the earth, and his eight books include *An Australian in America*; *La Cucina Italiana*; *The 100 Things Everyone Needs to Know About Australia*; and *The Obsessive Traveller, or Why I Don't Steal Towels From Great Hotels Any More*.

A traveller's alphabet of
Essential Places

David Dale

PICADOR
Pan Macmillan Australia

First published 1996 in Picador by Pan Macmillan Australia Pty Limited
St Martins Tower, 31 Market Street, Sydney

National Library of Australia
Cataloguing-in-Publication data:

Dale, David, 1948– .
A traveller's alphabet of essential places.

ISBN 0 330 35858 8.

1. Travel–Anecdotes. 2. Travel–Humour. I. Title

910.202

Typeset in 11/13 point Baskerville by Midland Typesetters
Printed in Australia by McPherson's Printing Group

CONTENTS

INTRODUCTION

There comes a moment in the life of every traveller when a terrible realisation strikes: there are only so many journeys left. The youthful notion that a lifetime is more than enough to see a whole world is replaced by the sense that your income and your holiday entitlements are going to keep you at home for most of every year. And that could mean you're looking forward to only 20 more voyages of discovery before you become too creaky to climb on a plane, train or donkey.

From this point onwards, you must make every journey count. So you start to reflect on why you go travelling at all. If your answer is 'for the scenery,' you'd better get a refund on this book right now, because that is not my answer. I reckon we travel to understand the world, and ultimately ourselves. The unexamined journey is not worth making. If reality imposes a limit on the time we can spend travelling, then we should be heading only for the places that will stimulate our imaginations. For me, that means where the world's biggest ideas were born—where somebody decided that the earth revolves around the sun, or that humans are descended from jellyfish, or that office blocks can be beautiful, or that communism works best when served with good food. These are the places that make your spine tingle as you stand in them, because you know something happened here that transformed the planet.

The Hindus use the word *darshana* for the mysterious ecstasy generated in the presence of a holy place. Modern western travellers may experience darshana under more secular conditions. The first time I felt it was in the flat of Sigmund Freud, in Vienna, when I realised that this room produced the most influential theory of the 20th century—that human behaviour is largely driven by the unconscious mind. The second time I felt darshana was inside El Transito synagogue, in Toledo, Spain, when I discovered that 600 years ago, Muslims, Jews and Christians gathered in this space to share their scientific discoveries in a triumph of human collaboration that has never been repeated.

I decided that from then on, I would travel in search of darshana, getting my ecstasy fixes in the places that generated this century's dominant imagery. And if I could enjoy, in the process, a couple of great meals, relaxing swims, train rides and even the odd view, so much the better. You are reading a progress report on a lifetime project.

The Hindus have another word, *pradakshina*, for the ritual of walking around a holy place and meditating on what it means. Using a broad definition of the word holy, I hope this book will help readers to engage in that ritual. I toyed with the idea of calling the book *Pradakshina*, but I didn't want to risk confusion with Shirley Maclaine's next autobiography. So I decided to name it for its content: the places that are essential for anyone who is excited by the world of ideas, the places that every thoughtful stay-at-home needs to know about and every passionate traveller needs to visit.

The destinations appear in alphabetical order, but it's not necessary to read the book that way. Many themes weave through the chapters, linking places, people, myths and theories in ways I hadn't even realised until I was well advanced in the writing. Sigmund Freud probably shared a table with Adolf Hitler in a Viennese cafe. Freud was obsessed with Tutankhamun's father. Charles Darwin wrote to Karl Marx. Vincent van Gogh painted the hills from which Nostradamus studied the stars. Albert Einstein wrote the theory of relativity in Prague and Zurich, but the manuscript ended up in Jerusalem. Woody Allen stayed in César Ritz's mansion in Paris. Frank Lloyd Wright designed the Blade Runner's apartment in Los Angeles.

You can treat this book as a collection of journeys through a landscape of ideas, and navigate in accordance with your particular interests. Here are some themes you could follow:

The political journey. This might begin in Chapter 4 with the Tolpuddle Martyrs, who discover trade unionism and are sent to Australia for their trouble. Also in that chapter, Karl Marx invents communism, but doesn't live to see its energising effect on Union Square, New York (Chapter 21), or its success in Bologna (2), or its collapse in Prague (16). Meanwhile nationalism inspires the struggles of Canada's Indians (17), the revolution that freed Greece from Turkey (9), the Nazi takeover of Vienna (5) and of the Ritz (18), and the push for California to secede from the United States (24). And in Chapter 26, Switzerland emerges as a model of political perfection.

The religious pilgrimage. This might begin in Chapter 22 when Tutankhamun's father decides that the world is run by one god rather than many. His monotheism doesn't stick, but a thousand years later the Jews take the ball and run with it through Chapter 10, where they are joined by the Christians and the Muslims. The Jews and Muslims come up against the Spanish Inquisition in Chapter 20, while Martin Luther starts reforming Christianity in Chapter 2. And polytheism makes a big comeback in Chapter 11.

The artistic journey. Vincent van Gogh finds his colours in Chapter 1; Hundertwasser splashes *his* colours all over Vienna in Chapter 6; Tutankhamun inspires the Nile Style in Chapter 22; Louis Sullivan turns skyscrapers into temples and Frank Lloyd Wright designs suburbia in Chapter 3; drug money makes Miami an architectural extravaganza (13); Andy Warhol sets up his Factory on Union Square (21); fung shui dictates the way Hong Kong looks (11) while Queensland just thinks BIG is beautiful (14); César Ritz perfects the art of hospitality (18); and a museum which walks the line between art and madness thrives in Switzerland (26).

The scientific investigation. Archimedes uses physics and geometry to defend Syracuse in Chapter 19; the Romans use his principles to build aqueducts in France and Spain in Chapter 23; Copernicus and Galileo turn the universe around in Chapter 2; Darwin turns humanity around in Chapter 4; and the spirit of Einstein finds rest in Jerusalem (10).

The psychoanalytic journey (or the Head Trip). Freud unearths the unconscious mind in Chapter 6; Jung extends it into a theory of myths and archetypes in Chapter 26; and Hollywood uses Jung to create the formula for a successful movie in Chapter 8. Meanwhile,

Jerusalem turns out to be a mental health hazard (10).

The sensual exploration. You might follow your nose to the perfume capital of the world in Chapter 7, and to the source of the world's most expensive wine in Chapter 25. The cultural importance of food fills Chapter 5 and reinforces Indian tribal identity in Chapter 17; Australia's gastronomic heart proves to be in Noosa (14); the political role of the palate becomes apparent in Bologna (2) and Cesar Ritz goes mad trying to satisfy all the senses in Chapter 18.

The musical progression. Venice celebrates Vivaldi's *Four Seasons* in Chapter 23; Smetana composes a river where Mozart met Casanova in Chapter 16; Don Maclean sings about Vincent (1) and Steve Martin sings about King Tut (22); there's a shrine to Elvis Presley in Miami (13); and Nellie Melba inspires a pudding in London (18).

The literary journey. Mark Twain tours the Holy Land in Chapter 10; Jane Austen and John Fowles haunt Lyme Regis (4); James Joyce passes Lenin in Zurich (26); Carl Hiassen and James Hall revel in Miami's crime (13) while Orson Welles feels the same way about Vienna (15); Vaclav Havel has to give up playwriting for politics (16); and William Randolph Hearst sells papers and buys Europe to build Xanadu (24).

Of course, you may simply be looking for a guidebook which describes the most interesting places to visit in a particular country. Then you could deconstruct *A Traveller's Alphabet of Essential Places* nation by nation:

France. You'll find Provence in Chapters 1 and 23; Paris in Chapters 5 (the restaurants), 18 (the best hotel) and 23 (the bridges); Grasse in 7; and Bordeaux in 25.

Italy. You'll find Bologna in Chapter 2; Rome and Florence in 5; Venice in Chapters 5, 18 and 23; Capri in 9; Orvieto, Assisi and Gubbio in 15; Sicily in 19.

The USA. Chicago is in Chapter 3; the food of New York, LA and Seattle is in 5; Hollywood is 8; Miami is 13; New York is 21; and California is 24.

England. Darwin's home, called Down House, is spelt differently from the neighbouring village of Downe and is in Chapter 4; so is Dorset. London's food is in 5.

China. Hong Kong's food is in Chapter 5; its belief system is in 11; and its best hotel is in 18.

Austria. Vienna is in Chapter 6; its alleged river is in 23; and its food is in 5.

Greece. The island of Hydra is in Chapter 9.

Vanuatu. Port Vila and Erakor are in Chapter 9.

Israel. Chapter 10 covers Jerusalem.

Switzerland. Chapter 12 is a journey down the Swiss spine from Zurich through Lucerne to Locarno; Lausanne's food is in 5 and its best hotel is in 18; and Zurich is 26.

Australia. The Sunshine Coast of Queensland is in Chapter 14.

The Czech Republic. Prague is Chapter 16 and its food is in 5.

Canada. British Columbia is in Chapter 17.

Spain. Toledo is in Chapter 20. The foods of Madrid and Segovia are in 5.

Egypt. Luxor is in Chapter 22. Cairo's food is in 5 and its river is in 23.

If jumping around like this sounds too complicated, start at Chapter 1 and read on. The patterns will become apparent.

There are 26 chapters in this book, but they contain reasons to be curious about some 35 destinations. Of course I am not claiming that these are the only essential places in the world. They happen to be 35 I have reached in 24 years of travelling. My next 30 years will be devoted to finding the others. If you know of any places which are essential because of what happened there—places that inspire darshana—please write and tell me about them, care of the publisher. My list grows longer every day.

Many people helped me to understand the places in this book. I am particularly grateful to Dr Lisa Ying for her insights into the customs and foodways of Hong Kong; Giampaolo Pertosi for the windows he opened onto Bologna; Fiona Williams for Dorset and Downe; Dr Bruce Kraig for Chicago; David Hay for Los Angeles; Phil and Jackie Jarratt for Queensland; Jill Ying for Seattle; Lino Mascolo for Capri; Bill Pownall and Francesca Meks-Taylor for Hydra; Michael Ekin Smyth for Vienna; Geraldine Brooks and Tony Horwitz for Cairo and Jerusalem; and Susan Anthony for Manhattan. Many books also guided me, and I have listed them near the index.

Friends who have read this manuscript tell me they can discern one more interconnecting pattern I didn't mention earlier. They see me getting married in Paris in Chapter 5 and honeymooning in Provence in Chapter 1. Then they see me taking my infant daughter for her first travel experience to Noosa in Chapter 14 and for the second and third journeys of her life to Dorset (4) and Rome (5). This book is dedicated to my favourite fellow travellers: Susan Williams and Amelia Dale. I may not get time to experience all the essential places that are still left to explore, but Amelia will.

I · ARLES, FRANCE

Vincent van Gogh arrived in Arles by train on 20 February 1888, in search of Japan. This piece of geographical eccentricity had a kind of logic to it. He'd become fascinated with Japanese prints. Since he couldn't afford to go that far south, he hoped the same kind of inspiration would be available in 'the south of France, the land of blue tones and gay colours'. Getting off the train in the middle of a snowstorm might have discouraged a lesser spirit, but he wrote to his sister soon afterwards: 'I don't need any Japanese prints, because I always say that I am in Japan right here. And therefore I only have to open my eyes and paint whatever is in front of my nose'.

I arrived in Arles by car with a new bride on a warm October evening, in search of three things: (1) a decent cheap hotel; (2) a genuine aioli; and (3) an explanation of how Provence turned Vincent van Gogh into the most familiar artist of the 20th century. When he was in

Holland, Vincent painted in murky browns—a depressing scene called *The Potato Eaters*, from 1885, is typical. But within days of arriving in Arles he exploded in reds and blues and yellows, turning out joyous landscapes and glowing interiors and what came to be the most expensive pictures in human history—*Irises* ($79 million), *Sunflowers* ($58 million) and *The Trinquetalle Bridge* ($29 million). There have been many attempted explanations—a disease of the retina, schizophrenic hallucinations, epilepsy, a sedative called potassium bromide, too much absinthe making his heart grow fonder. None of them rings true.

For us in the 20th century, Vincent van Gogh is the archetype of The Artist. To be truly great, The Artist must: (a) starve in squalor; (b) be passionate to the point of madness; (c) barely survive several suicide attempts; and (d) be misunderstood in his lifetime but admired by later generations. Don Maclean sold that myth to a mass audience in the hit song *Starry Starry Night*, telling us about paintings of 'flaming flowers that brightly blaze, swirling clouds in violet haze, reflecting Vincent's eyes of China blue' and 'how you suffered for your sanity, how you tried to set them free. They would not listen, they did not know how, perhaps they'll listen now'. All this started in Arles in 1888, which makes it an essential place.

Part 1 of my quest resolved itself when I had to turn into a driveway to avoid being hit by a truck reversing out of a traffic jam. The driveway belonged to the Hotel d'Arlatan, which proved to be a higgledy-piggledy structure full of irrelevant staircases and tiny rooms with floral wallpaper and creaky beds. We dumped our bags, then set off on The Quest, part 2.

In English-speaking countries, we tend to think of aioli as a mayonnaise into which we dip our chips at bistros. In Provence, at least historically, aioli is an entire meal. It's a wide shallow dish of steamed seasonal vegetables, sometimes with snails or a lump of fish, covered with creamy waves of a sauce made from eggs, olive oil and a lot of crushed garlic. (There is a peculiarly Provençal technique for getting the skin off the garlic. Put the garlic clove on a wooden board and then thump it, just once, with the heel of your hand. It's called 'the Provençal Slap'. You'll find that the skin now falls away easily from the flesh—of the garlic, not your hand.) I had arrived in the heartland of aioli and I was ready for it.

At night, Arles is sinister. It's a labyrinth of grey buildings, narrow winding lanes and minimal lighting, where you can wander for minutes at a time without seeing another soul and then feel you should hurry past them when you do. The centre of Arles must have been livelier in Vincent's time, buzzing with the sound of bars and brothels.

A cold wind was starting to slice round the corners as we stepped into a little square. Then came a thrill of recognition. We were looking at the inspiration for a painting called *The Cafe Terrace on the Place du Forum, Arles, at Night,* done by Vincent in September 1888 when he was in cheerful mood, expecting a visit from his friend Gaugin (and when he painted *Sunflowers,* to hang in Gaugin's bedroom). But there were a few differences. Vincent's cafe glowed with welcoming yellow light. These days Snack Bar le Paris is neon lit and more like a hangout for bikies than bohemians. Vincent's cobbles have been replaced by tar, there's a big dark statue in the middle of the square, and the stars in the night sky must have shrunk since last century. But my scalp was tingling with the knowledge that my feet were on a spot where Vincent had placed his easel.

The aioli proved more elusive. In a restaurant called La Gueule du Loup, which had been recommended by previous travellers, we asked if there were any regional dishes. The waitress replied: 'You won't find any of that here—just good food'. That point became debatable as we tried to extract some flavour from the chicken and mushrooms (with noodles) and the wild pig in red wine which the waitress had suggested. She was not, I hasten to say, a Provençal person. She told us she was born in Australia but was married to a French chef.

I'd been worried that Provence would be overrun with tweedy English types trying to find the footprints of Peter Mayle, but the English were not the problem. If anyone's ruining Provence, it's the French. In my movements round the south I'd found that rural restaurateurs, looking for extra stars from the Michelin guide, were discarding their booming flavours, bright colours and seasonal variations and were refining their dishes into what they imagined to be the current Paris vogue. As a result, *le vrai aioli* was an endangered species. I fell asleep grumpy in my creaking bed that night.

The Place du Forum looked a lot brighter next morning, with locals taking coffee in the middle. The dark statue turned out to be Frédéric Mistral, a mustachioed poet who was whipping up regionalism in Arles during Vincent's time. Mistral wanted Provence to return to the glorious Middle Ages, when it produced the most talented troubadours in Europe. He insisted on speaking an ancient dialect called Oc. The name of the dialect came from the southern way of saying the word for yes, which is 'oui' to the northern French. Oc speakers also say 'lou' instead of 'le'. So if Mistral had run into Vincent, who spoke northern French with a Dutch accent, neither would have understood much of the conversation. In 1904 Mistral won the Nobel Prize for literature and used the prize money to set up a regional museum. He also started a magazine devoted to promoting local culture. He called the magazine *Aioli* in honour of the national dish of Provence, which, he said, 'heats up the body and bathes the soul in rapture'.

I was carrying with me a Baedecker guide to southern France from the year 1907, which was the closest I could get to a description of the area as Vincent van Gogh would have known it. Baedecker made this observation: 'The women of Arles are famed for their good looks (Greek type) and tasteful costume, with its chappelle (white fichu) and black velvet head dress'. I fell into disputation with an elderly woman dressed this way when I tried to enter Mistral's museum (called Lou Museon Arlaten in Oc dialect). Addressing me in northern French as a big favour, she said she would not sell me a ticket because it was 11.30 am. Since the Museon closed for lunch at noon, I would not have time to see it properly. When I swore I'd be finished in half an hour, she took offence at my superficiality but threw me a ticket and then insisted on trailing close behind me to ensure I was keeping up the pace. (After dealing with her, I understood Vincent's observation in a letter to his brother Theo: 'It is a filthy town this, with the old streets. As for the women of Arles ... they are no longer what they must have been'.)

The Museon includes illustrations of how to tie your shawl in the correct regional way; dusty samples of locally made furniture; pottery; paisley material; the cradle in which Frédéric Mistral was rocked as a child; and two weird dioramas, one showing peasants welcoming a newborn baby with gifts, and the other showing Christmas dinner in a farmhouse (without aioli). So I was looking at scenes of Arles as it was in Vincent's day, but the colours were greys and pastels. Nothing in the Museon looked like Vincent's paintings. The same discrepancy struck me as I strolled through the ancient Roman cemetery called the Alyscamps (a word which looks like a synonym for street urchins, but actually is the local name for *champs elysees*, or Elysian fields). Vincent painted the Alyscamps repeatedly, with red footpaths, orange trees and blue or green tombs. To my eyes, the Alyscamps are light brown and silvery green and grey.

Next stop was the hospital where Vincent was treated after he threatened to attack Gaugin (who proved to be an obnoxious guest), then cut off his own earlobe and presented it, gift wrapped, to a prostitute named Rachel, asking her to 'guard this object carefully'. (This action displayed the same sort of logic as going to Arles to find Japan— Vincent was emulating the actions of the bullfighters he used to watch every Sunday in the Arles amphitheatre; they would cut off the bull's ear and present it as a trophy to their loved one. Various humanitarians at the time were campaigning against bullfighting, but Frédéric Mistral organised a counter-campaign, on the theory that *tauromachie* was essential to Provençal culture. The fights in the amphitheatre continue to this day.)

Here was my biggest surprise: the hospital looked just like the painting Vincent did in April 1889—white balconies with blue and orange trim, hedges dotted with red and yellow flowers—everything identical, right down to the lilies in the pond. So Vincent's art was just a rendition of real colours after all? No. The explanation: the hospital is now an office complex called Espace van Gogh, which was meticulously redecorated in the 1980s to conform with Vincent's painting. Life has replicated art.

The Vincent trail led onwards, by a half hour drive, to the town of St Remy and the St Paul mental hospital. This was where Vincent admitted himself after the citizens of Arles took up a petition against him. It's still a clinic, and the doors are barred to sightseers, so you can't look out the window of the first floor bedroom from which Vincent painted *Starry Night* (and which was later occupied by Albert Schweitzer, the medical missionary and philosopher, when German prisoners were interned in the hospital during World War I). But you can stand in the olive orchard and look at trees which were already old when Vincent painted them in June 1889. Soon after entering the asylum, he wrote to Theo: 'The olive trees are very characteristic and I long to tackle them. It is a silver, sometimes blue, sometimes greenish, bronzy, paling on yellower ground, rose violet or orangey through to dead red ochre. But difficult, very difficult, drawing me to work entirely in gold and silver'. Walk in the surrounding scrubby hills and you can see many of Vincent's inspirations and smell the sage, rosemary and lavender that grows wild there.

St Remy's major industry these days, I suspect, is directing pilgrims to the St Paul asylum. Back in 1907, before the world had discovered Vincent, the Baedecker guidebook described St Remy thus: 'an unimportant town of 6000 inhab., with tree shaded boulevards; contains an imposing modern church with a Gothic belfry of 1330 . . . Beyond St Remy the countryside is uninteresting'. Now, of course, that countryside is just the opposite, because it was colourised by Vincent, idealised by Peter Mayle, and romanticised by the movies *My Mother's Castle* and *My Father's Glory*, based on books by Marcel Pagnol.

St Remy has a magnificent open-air market on Saturday morning, with rows of stalls displaying herbs and mushrooms, so I had high hopes of regional eating. And I did find an aioli, though not The Aioli. It was in an elegant restaurant called Le Marceau. The dinner included the most delicate pizza I have ever eaten: a thin crunchy crust covered with slim slices of tomato, basil and anchovy (which I decided to count as local cuisine, since the concept of pizza supposedly developed from a Provençal dish called *pissaladiera*). The aioli was so polite it was hardly noticeable: carved pieces of fennel, celery, carrot, potato and cauliflower, a quail egg, and a dollop of bright yellow mayonnaise. If there was garlic in it, my palate was too jaded to notice.

Round the corner from Le Marceau, in Rue Hoche, you encounter a blackened two-storey house which was the birthplace of another visionary who attracted his biggest audience in the 20th century—Michel de Notredame, aka Nostradamus. Like Vincent, Nostradamus had hallucinations. He exorcised the demons not through painting but through poetry.

Michel de Notredame was born in 1503 into a family of Jews who had converted to avoid the Inquisition (see Chapter 20). He studied the starry nights from the hills round St Remy to develop his skills as an astrologer, then trained as a doctor. He invented a potion that supposedly cured the Plague, and he wrote the world's first book of recipes for jams and jellies, but neither of those achievements is what he's remembered for. The books that made a difference were his collections of four-line verses, which have been taken by wishful thinkers over the centuries to be harbingers of global events. Catherine de Medici paid him a fortune to describe her future, so Nostradamus was rich when he died at his house in the village of Salon (worth a detour on the way back from St Remy to Arles). On the evening of 1 July 1566, his assistant farewelled him with the words: 'Tomorrow, master'. Nostradamus replied: 'Tomorrow at sunrise, I shall no longer be here'. The next morning he was found dead from an attack of dropsy.

Vincent could confidently have made the same prediction on the night of 28 July 1890. After a year in the St Remy asylum, he returned to the north in May 1890, settling in a town called Auvers, near Paris. His paintings grew darker and drabber, with the magnificent exception of the blues, reds and yellows of *Wheat Field With Crows*. On 27 July he borrowed a revolver and headed off into those wheat fields, saying he wanted to shoot some crows, and shot himself in the chest. Then he walked back to his attic room above the Café Ravoux, despairing that he couldn't even make a success of suicide. Two days later he died.

Back in Arles, we weren't contemplating such drastic action, but we were wishing for the services of Nostradamus as we systematically combed the old town, examining all the menus outside eating places. Most were full of current Parisian fads such as salmon tartare and foie gras and magret de canard. But finally, on the door of a crowded and noisy cafe near the Roman amphitheatre, we saw scribbled on a piece of cardboard the words 'Aioli 55F'. The place was called l'Escaladou (Provençal for 'the staircase'). From a blackboard menu we ordered just two dishes: *poularde*—which proved to be a gigantic casserole of chicken, tomato and carrots with a bowl of rice—and the aioli.

The aioli was a shock. The vegetables were green beans, cauliflower, potatoes and carrots, all cooked quite a bit more than is the Paris fashion. They were nuzzling up to a lump of bony white fish. The mayonnaise that sprawled across them was a raging beast. It was just olive oil, beaten egg yolks, a bit of mustard and a tonne of mashed raw garlic, but overpowering doesn't begin to describe it. One spoonful, I suspected, could wake the dead. My eyes were watering, either with agony or ecstasy. I never thought there could be such a thing as too much garlic, but it was around my mouth and emerging from my skin and filling my brain with fiendish visions for three days afterwards.

And as I ate it, I had a revelation. I had already established that Vincent van Gogh's colours didn't come from the Provençal countryside. They came from inside him. And what else was inside him? What must he have been eating almost every day? Think of how he painted the source of olive oil outside the asylum. Think of *Starry Night*. What are those fat white swirling stars if not knobs of garlic? Think of *The Reaper*, a canvas overflowing with golden waves of mayonnaise.

Aioli as Vincent's hallucinogen? Remember Mistral's words: 'it heats up the body and bathes the soul in rapture'. If you find my theory fanciful, try this test: beat together two egg yolks, two cups of olive oil, a splash of lemon juice and 10 garlic cloves which you have skinned (using the Provençal Slap) and mashed in a mortar with a bit of sea salt. Pour the mixture over boiled potatoes, artichokes and carrots, and eat. Wait half an hour and start turning the pages of a book of Vincent's paintings. I rest my case.

2 · BOLOGNA, ITALY

The two towers at the end of Via Rizzoli stand—or rather, lean—as a permanent reminder to the citizens of Bologna of the folly of competition. The story goes that the right-hand tower was started by the Asinelli family in the year 1109, and when their great rivals, the Garisenda family, saw it rising, they set about building a taller one next to it. Each time one family went higher, the other family went higher still—but then the Garisenda tower started tilting (skyscraper technology not being quite as reliable in 12th century Italy as it became in 19th century Chicago; see Chapter 3). Still, brick after brick, generation after generation, the families kept up their race. Finally the top of the Garisenda tower became so precarious that the city authorities ordered the family to lop it off. Today the Garisenda is just a stump, 48 metres tall, while the Asinelli reaches 98 metres but looks as if it could topple over at any minute. As the Bolognese will tell you, if the families had only been able to cooperate, there would probably be one good upright tower in the city today.

The Asinelli tower is unlikely to fall down just yet, so you should climb the 486 steps inside it and clamber out onto its top. From there you will see an instructive panorama—the red-roofed houses of a city of 450,000 people, surrounded by lush green meadows and low hills. You might imagine that the pinky-orange buildings are the reason Bologna is known throughout Italy as *la rossa* ('the red one') and that may once have been the explanation. But nowadays, Bologna is known as 'the red one' for another reason: in every election since 1946 it has chosen a communist city council, and when the communist party dissolved itself in 1990, the Bolognese kept electing the same people under their new name, the Democratic Party of the Left. The lesson of the two towers has settled deep into the Bolognese mind.

Bologna has many other nicknames. It's called *la grassa*, which means 'the fat one'. The view from the top of the Torre Asinelli explains that as well. The green fields surrounding the town are part of the richest agricultural area in Italy, producing wheat for pasta, rice for risotto, grapes for wine, pigs for sausages, and cattle for butter, cream, cheese and beef. The Emilia-Romagna region, of which Bologna is the capital, is legendary for both the quality and the quantity of its eating habits. The great celebrator of fleshy pleasures, Boccaccio, writing *The Decameron* in the 14th century, described a land where 'there is a mountain consisting entirely of grated parmesan, on which live people who do nothing but cook macaroni and ravioli in chicken broth, which they roll down the slopes so that it arrives at the bottom coated with fragrant cheese'. Boccaccio called the land Utopia, but everyone knew he was talking about Emilia-Romagna.

We can say that Bologna is the only successful blend of communism and hedonism in the history of the world. It remains virtually unknown to tourists because it is too busy going about its business to bother trying to attract them. But in Italy it is the envy of every other city. They envy the way Bologna eats. They envy the way Bologna runs—its local government is the least corrupt and least inefficient in the country. And they envy the way Bologna makes love—or at least, how they imagine it makes love. Bologna has a reputation for sensuality which the locals say they have trouble living up to.

The first time I was planning a visit, I asked a group of Romans to tell me about the city. They started chuckling and doing the Italian equivalent of 'nudge, nudge, wink, wink'. One of them told me to be sure to try the local specialty, *bocchini* (pronounced bok-eeny). 'Is it a form of pasta?' I asked. That sent them into hysterics. One of them, an Alitalia pilot, told me it was airline policy not to fly over Bologna because of the strong downwards suction in the air currents from the city. I began to get the idea. Finally somebody whispered: 'Bocchini means blowjob. The prostitutes in Bologna give the best blowjobs in Italy. They practise on the university students'. (I am unable to confirm this, although I can vouch for the tortellini.)

In 1995, an opinion poll asked residents of Bologna to indicate their level of satisfaction with the quality of their life. The result was 50.8 percent describing themselves as 'very satisfied', and a further 43.5 percent saying 'satisfied enough'. I can't think of another city in the world which could inspire such a response from its citizens.

Partly by myth and partly by reality, Bologna has become a model for the aspirations of all Italians. But envy can turn to jealousy—Bologna makes some Italians angry. In 1980 a bomb went off at Bologna railway station, killing 85 people and injuring 200 others. At first it was blamed on the Red Brigades, who were supposedly trying to punish la rossa for not being red enough. Then the truth emerged: the bomb had been planted by a group of right-wing extremists connected to the Christian Democrat Party, who feared that Bologna was giving communism such a good name that voters in the rest of Italy might go the same way.

The fascists' fears were confirmed in 1996, when the Olive Tree Coalition became the government of Italy. That coalition was planted and nurtured in Emilia-Romagna. The man chosen as Italy's Prime Minister, Romano Prodi, was born in Bologna and headed an economic think-tank there. The choice of name for his grouping of former communists, socialists, and progressive Christian Democrats was a brilliant piece of marketing, and typically Bolognese. Italians can't help but respond favourably to the symbolism of olive oil—full flavoured, all natural, likely to reduce heart disease and cancer, and with a tradition going back to the glories of ancient Rome.

A closer look at some of Bologna's nicknames might help to explain the success of its thousand-year social experiment . . .

La dotta, which means 'the learned one'. Europe's oldest university started in Bologna in 1088, and the spirit of scepticism and inquiry that it encouraged has made the city a bastion of radical thought ever since. Copernicus, a Pole by origin, studied at Bologna University in 1496 and went on to theorise that the sun rather than the earth was the centre of the universe. (He got away with it because he wasn't Italian. When Galileo proved Copernicus right in 1632, he was forced to recant by the

Italian Inquisition—but they were in Rome, not Bologna.)

Legend has it that Bologna was also where the Reformation began. A monk called Martin Luther was supposedly standing in Bologna's Basilica of San Petronio in 1530 watching the Pope crown Charles V of Germany as Holy Roman Emperor, when he became so disgusted with the pomp and pageantry that he decided to rebel against the notion that the Pope was God's representative on earth. Protestants the world over should make Bologna their Mecca.

Over the centuries, Bologna university has educated the likes of Thomas Becket, Dante, Petrarch, Boccaccio, Rossini, Marconi and Umberto Eco, who now teaches there. At the time of Martin Luther's visit, the university had 10,000 students. Now it has 80,000, and if you stroll along Via Zamboni (which leads from the square containing the two leaning towers) you'll feel as if all 80,000 of them are cramming its cafes or sticking posters on its walls or lounging in its doorways. Professor Fabio Roversi-Monaco, who rejoices in the title *Il Magnifico Rettore* ('the magnificent rector') of the university, explains the wealth, prestige and social progressiveness of Bologna entirely by the presence of the university: 'Bologna is Bologna only because of the university and that has been true for nine centuries'.

La citta dei portici, which means 'the city of porticoes'. Central Bologna has 35 kilometres of colonnades, the result of an accommodation crisis when the university's numbers began to grow in the 14th century. Because they couldn't expand outside the walls, the citizens of Bologna built enclosed balconies onto their upper floors, which stretched over the footpaths below. The long galleries let you walk almost anywhere in Bologna's centre without getting sunburnt or rained on, and they give the city a sense of enclosure and intimacy, as if you're inside somebody's home even when you're in the street. Around 7 p.m. is the time of *passagiata*, when the locals stroll along the colonnades arm in arm, involved in intense conversation or just showing off their latest acquisitions from the posh clothing stores.

La citta delle belle donne, which means 'the city of the beautiful women'. It's a euphemism that suggests Bologna's reputation as the sex capital of Italy. The locals do nothing to discourage the image, holding annual festivals of erotica and even giving their streets such names as Vicolo Baciadame ('lady kisser lane') and Via Fregatette ('rub tits street').

Pope John Paul II clearly believed the stereotype of Bologna, because he issued a judgement known as an anathema on the city, condemning its pursuit of godless sensuality. The local archbishop, Giacomo Biffi, is trying to introduce an annual day devoted to celebrating the virtues of virginity. Biffi is one of the most conservative cardinals in Italy (and one of the last to believe the Shroud of Turin is genuine). He says he has to lead the fightback for morality 'in an era dominated by a culture which considers sex as an absolute right above the law'. The Bolognese find Biffi very entertaining, and will proudly tell you that he is a prime candidate to become the next pope—which would mean that Bologna could control both the secular and the religious politics of the nation.

La rossa. It is usually argued that Bologna went for licentiousness and socialism as a reaction against being ruled by the Popes for 350 years. During the early Renaissance, Bologna was a proud self-governing city-state. Then the Vatican took it over in 1506, appointing governors from among the local rich. When Bologna gained its freedom as part of united Italy in 1860, there was a lot of resentment waiting to burst out. Italian socialism was born there in 1861, with the formation of the first Workers' Society, and in 1914 Bologna elected its first socialist mayor. During World War II the city was split between the fascists and the communist-led partisans. When the Allied forces arrived in 1945, Bologna had already been liberated by the partisans, and in the 1946 elections, the communists gained the control they have held ever after.

Bolognese-style communism was at first Stalinist and puritanical, but from 1956, when they learned what Stalin was really like, the Bolognese communists opened up, and have been in the forefront of liberal reform since then. To help mothers go to work, the council set up an extensive system of childcare centres and pre-schools. It started a chain of chemist shops to make medicines available at low prices. It made public transport in the inner city free during peak hours. It provided services for the elderly that included low-rent housing, free taxis, home-help and subsidised holidays. It preserved the historic centre by making many streets pedestrian-only and by renovating the most ancient buildings to become community housing rather than sterile tourist sites.

At the same time the council went out of its way to dispel the myth that communism was anti-capitalist, by encouraging the growth of small businesses, sometimes family owned and sometimes run by workers' cooperatives. And because industry, especially the food industry, is so successful in Bologna, the council could charge high property taxes and use the money to improve social services.

When I first visited Bologna in 1982, a local journalist took me to watch the mayor, Renato Zangheri, performing that day's official function. The journalist told me

Zangheri was a skilful politician who had made the Catholic Church his ally, and the party bosses at communist headquarters wanted him to move to Rome to lead the party in the national elections. They thought he had the charisma to make him Italy's first communist prime minister.

The function that day turned out to be handing over one of the city's renovated buildings to be used as offices for an organisation called ARCI-Gay, which represents what the Italians call 'politicised homosexuals'. At the handover ceremony, the leader of ARCI-Gay kissed Mayor Zangheri on the lips, and a photo of this appeared on the front page of the local paper the next day. Church officials muttered disapprovingly, but Mayor Zangheri handled the incident with his usual humour, declaring in a press statement that he and his wife were glad the gay activists were grateful for the city's assistance, but a simple handshake would suffice in future. The exercise showed a public relations skill which seemed typically Bolognese. When AIDS became an issue in the mid-1980s, Bologna was the first city in Italy to issue condoms to prisoners in its jail and to introduce AIDS testing for women in the first three months of pregnancy. (Renato Zangheri never did move to Rome; he said he liked living in Bologna too much.)

In 1988 Bologna invited Alexander Dubcek, the former leader of Czechoslovakia, to receive an honorary degree at the university. It was a piece of mischief designed to embarrass the Czech Government, which could hardly stop one of its citizens from being honoured by another communist government. The invitation told the world that Bologna's sympathies lay with the freedoms Dubcek briefly introduced before the Soviet tanks crushed the Prague Spring of 1968 (see Chapter 16).

Putting himself at considerable risk once he returned to Prague, Dubcek told the cheering Bolognese: 'For a man who has been considered to be on the margins of society, to be unexpectedly called by the world's oldest university for a recognition that belies all that, could hardly do other than provoke a series of tumultuous emotions'. Dubcek recognised that Bologna's communism was unique, but if he had been able to continue the changes he was introducing in 1968, Prague might have become Bologna's twin city, another example to the world that socialism does not have to be joyless. 'Without outside intervention, our efforts would have been crowned with success,' Dubcek said. 'The intervention was a serious error. It was carried out to suffocate the experiment we had started.' He said that in Czechoslovakia, the two decades since 1968 had seen 'the worsening of economic stagnation, sterility and incalculable moral losses'. Dubcek was vindicated a year later when Czech communism self-destructed.

In 1990, delegates representing the 1.4 million members of Italy's Communist Party met in Bologna, sang *The Red Flag* for the last time, pulled down the hammer and sickle signs and voted their party out of existence. Communism had become irrelevant to modern times, they said. Bologna elected a strangely familiar group called the Democratic Party of the Left to continue where the communists had left off.

The council's latest advance has been a move into computerisation, which has made Bologna largely free of the red tape that strangles most Italian cities. Now you don't have to queue for hours or bribe a bunch of clerks to obtain a copy of your birth certificate or car registration papers or other necessary documents. You just type your requirements into a kind of automatic teller machine in the wall in central Bologna and it will spit out the papers within a minute. The city has also set up a system whereby citizens with computers can be connected for free to the Internet. The project is called NetTuno, a nice pun since King Neptune, the central figure of the Fontana del Nettuno in the main square, is the symbol of Bologna. Typically, the city council sees two advantages to linking its citizens into the World Wide Web: it offers 'a new model for participatory democracy' and it helps Bolognese businesses sell their products to the world.

The council has also been concerned lately that Bologna might fall victim to the racism that seems to be growing in other Italian cities. To show its citizens that they should not feel superior to the Africans who are starting to do some of the menial work in the city, the council invited Moussa Sow, an anthropologist from Mali, to study life in Bologna for five months. He concluded that women were in command of the society, children were spoilt, and too much money was spent on housing and food. He said Africans would find Europe 'a desperately sad place' but the 'tortellini-adoring tribe' had a 'surprising elegance' that lifted them above other Europeans.

La grassa. Different areas of Italy favour different cooking mediums—some use olive oil, some butter, and some fat. Bologna uses all three, and particularly the last two. Its food is the richest and heaviest in the country, which the Bolognese rationalise by saying they work the hardest. The traditional specialities are *mortadella*, a spiced pork sausage that was the symbol of the Guild of Sausage Makers formed in Bologna in 1376; *tortellini*, little doughnuts of pasta stuffed with seasoned pork, veal and cheese and supposedly modelled in the 14th century on the shape of a woman's navel; and *lasagna*, sheets of pasta interleaved with meat sauce and cheese, which seems to date to several centuries BC, when it was called *laganum*.

All of these and much more are on display in the lavish food stores that line the lanes around the Piazza Maggiore, and in restaurants such as Pappagallo, Diana and Rosteria Luciano. But the visitor to Bologna will search in vain for spaghetti bolognese, which seems to be an American invention that has returned to haunt the kind of Italian restaurants that specialise in tour-bus groups. The nearest thing to it in Bologna is *tagliatelle al ragu*—flat noodles with a concentrated sauce of onions, carrots, pork, veal, butter and tomato.

After you have spent a few days eating in Bologna (and realising the value of siesta for recovering after lunch) you might reduce the city's secret of success to this formula: if people are well fed, they will be happy. So they will work hard and they will become rich. And they will want to share their happiness with people less fortunate, to cooperate rather than compete, to be generous rather than selfish, to be adventurous rather than restrictive in their social ideas.

Does Bologna have any flaws? Possibly a complacency, an insularity, a smugness which you can't help sensing in any prolonged conversation with a Bolognese. As Italy's Prime Minister, Romano Prodi, says: 'We Bolognese still see ourselves in terms of the old stereotypes. We believe we are superior in everything—food, elegance, good looks, friendliness. But is it true?'

It's hard not to answer yes to Prodi's question. So what do we learn from the Bologna model? If you want to create Utopia, put your city in the middle of a rich agricultural area; make good eating a priority for everyone; set up a large university and allow it freedom of thought; spend 1000 years building and preserving a historic centre; let workers band together to improve their conditions, run their own businesses, and form a political party; and have your city regularly criticised by religious conservatives so that your citizens can enjoy a satisfying sense of boldness. What could be simpler?

3 · CHICAGO, USA

In the dining room of Frank Lloyd Wright's house in Oak Park, Chicago, the chairs have straight backs that are so tall they rise well over the heads of those who sit in them. Even the baby's high chair has the same tall stiff back. There's a reason for this, and it isn't comfort (Wright said himself that he was 'black and blue' from sitting in his own furniture). He designed the chairs so that the family using them would be forced into togetherness. The high backs create an extra wall—a room within a room to enclose the family round the table. With chairs like this, there can be no question of anyone sitting back and opting out of the conversation.

For the same reason, Wright designed a servery in the wall through which his servants could push the plates of food, so that they didn't need to enter the dining room and disrupt family discussions. The food itself would also be no distraction—as plain as could be, with 'codfish, salt pork and bananas' being Wright's favourites, and only water to drink rather than such artificial stimulants as alcohol, coffee or tea.

When the family left the dining room, they gathered round a huge fireplace, over which Wright put two possibly contradictory slogans: 'Truth is life' and 'Good friend, around these hearth stones speak no evil words of any creature'. To Wright, the hearth was even more important than the dining room, and he tried to include one in every house he designed.

The most influential architect of the 20th century believed in the family, which must be why he had so many of them. In 1909 he left his wife Kitty and their six children in the house in Oak Park and ran off with the wife of one of his clients—Mamah (pronounced mayma) Cheney. He built a new house, called Taliesin, in Wisconsin, and moved in with her. But in August 1914 he came up against someone who believed in family values even more than he did. While Wright was away designing an amusement park in Chicago, a servant named Julian Carlton put an axe through Mamah Cheney's head, murdered six other people who were staying with her, and set fire to Taliesin. The reason given for the murder was that Carlton, a religious man, had gone mad when he learned his master and mistress were not married.

The following year, Wright began an affair with a socialite named Miriam Noel, whom he had met after she wrote him a fan letter. They married as soon as Kitty granted him a divorce in 1922, but Wright left home six months after the ceremony, and began an affair with Olgivanna Hinzenburg, a married woman with a seven-year-old daughter. She was 26 and he was 57. In 1925 she bore another daughter and the four of them moved into the rebuilt Taliesin.

Miriam Noel started a legal action against Olgivanna

for 'alienation of affections', and Olgivanna's husband sued Wright for abducting his daughter. Wright and his new family 'disappeared' in mid-1926, with detectives and journalists pursuing them through hotel rooms all over America. Wright was arrested in October, and spent two nights in jail before his friends and lawyers could begin the process of extricating him from the mess. Miriam Noel granted him a divorce in 1927, and he married Olgivanna in 1928. Miriam Noel went insane and died in hospital in 1930 of what the medical certificate called 'exhaustion following delirium'.

The guides who take you through Wright's house in Oak Park are under orders not to mention any of this stuff, and they change the subject when you ask about it. They only want to tell you that Wright used the house as his design laboratory for the first ten years of his career, rebuilding it every few months, and that of the 440 Wright projects that were actually built, 126 were planned in the Oak Park house or the attached studio. The guide managed to distract me for a minute from questions about Wright's family life by pointing to the old desk of an employee named Walter Burley Griffin and leaving me to speculate that the first plans for the city of Canberra may have been drawn on that surface.

The most personal the guide was prepared to get was pointing to Wright's passport from 1905, which is framed on a bedroom wall. His description reads: 'Height: 5 foot 8½. Forehead: sloping. Eyes: brown. Nose: large. Mouth: not large. Chin: regular. Hair: dark. Face: smooth shaven.' I wondered aloud whether this could account for his appeal to women. The guide didn't smile.

So I was unable to solve the mystery of how, through 20 years of the most agonising emotional and legal turbulence, Frank Lloyd Wright was able to establish a reputa/tion as the greatest architect in America. Not that he was satisfied with such faint praise. When an art historian described him in 1930 as 'the greatest architect and perhaps the greatest American of the early 20th century', Wright responded: 'Having a good start, not only do I fully intend to be the greatest architect who has yet lived—but the greatest architect who will ever live.'

For one of his last projects—a graceful little skyscraper in the town of Bartlesville, Oklahoma—Wright instructed that a quote from the poet Walt Whitman be emblazoned in the lobby: 'Where the city that has produced the greatest man stands, There the greatest city stands'. If that is true, then the greatest city must be Chicago, because it produced not only Frank Lloyd Wright but five more generations of innovators who have been coming ever closer to seizing his crown.

People make the pilgrimage to Chicago for many good reasons other than Wright. It has produced America's finest hotdogs, best pizzas, roughest politics, most flamboyant gangsters, most powerful blues music and cleverest comedic improvisers (its Second City Theatre trained Alan Alda, Alan Arkin, Dan Aykroyd, John Belushi, John Candy, Elaine May, Harold Ramis and many others). But what makes Chicago essential is that it gave birth to the symbol of the 20th century—the skyscraper. And having created the world's first skyscrapers in the 1880s and the world's best skyscrapers in the 1920s, it has kept generating America's most exciting constructions ever since.

When gothic towers were the fad, Chicago built the Wrigley Building (1922), as white and twisty as the chewing gum that financed it, and the Tribune Tower (1925), the winning entry in a competition to design 'the most beautiful and distinctive office building in the world'. That was a decade when money seemed limitless, and the Chicago high-rises crawled with gargoyles, mosaics, battlements and buttresses. When 'less is more' became the prevailing philosophy in the 1950s, Chicago architects produced structures of austere elegance, while cities with narrower vision and shorter pockets ended up with a bland bunch of cornflake boxes. When 'postmodern' playfulness became the style of the 1980s, Chicago architects led the way with taste and humour. Its new office blocks sprouted pink and green patches and Greek temples and mock cottages and pyramid hats. And again, the world followed—not always successfully.

Chicago can not only build high-rises but can display them to best advantage. New York might boast about the Flatiron, the Chrysler and the Empire State, but try getting a decent perspective on those monoliths in the narrow canyons of Gotham. In Chicago you have the river and the lake to provide vistas of glittering spires. The 1920s masterpieces surround you, for example, if you stand on the bridge over the Chicago River at Michigan Avenue (which also happens to be the site of Fort Dearborn, Chicago's first European settlement in 1679).

How did this city's 100-year passion for adventurous building come about? It seems that the Great Fire of 1871 was the best thing that ever happened to Chicago, because it provided a clean slate on which the merchant princes of America's midwest could erect monuments to their own wealth. To sculpt these temples of capitalism, they hired the boldest spirits in the new profession of architecture. And two technological advances gave those spirits the chance to soar—steel frameworks on which tall buildings could be hung, and electric elevators to save the inhabitants' legs.

One of these newly arrived design pioneers was Louis

Sullivan, who became the father of the skyscraper and the mentor of Frank Lloyd Wright. When Wright was working as a draftsman in Sullivan's studio in 1889, he witnessed the moment of conception. Sullivan had been commissioned to design the first office block for the town of St Louis, and had gone for a walk to think about the best way to accommodate a large number of workers. Suddenly he burst back into the studio, and finished the sketch in a few minutes. Wright said later: 'I was perfectly aware of what had happened. This was Louis Sullivan's greatest moment—his greatest effort. The "skyscraper" as a new thing under the sun, an entity with beauty all its own, was born.'

Sullivan not only designed skyscrapers, he argued the case for them with the conservative establishment that controlled architecture outside Chicago. In his 1896 book, *The Tall Office Building Artistically Considered*, he coined the phrase 'form ever follows function', meaning that a building's shape should reflect its intended use. A tall office building ought to be 'based exactly on the practical necessities, but expressed with a sentiment of largeness and freedom,' Sullivan said. He did not intend form follows function to become an excuse for the mass production of ugly boxes. 'We are on the high road to a natural and satisfying art,' he wrote, 'an architecture that will soon become a fine art in the true, the best sense of the word, an art that will be of the people, for the people and by the people.' Ultimately it was Wright who travelled furthest down that road.

The world's oldest surviving skyscraper is in Chicago, of course, but it is not one of Sullivan's. It is the Manhattan Building at 431 South Dearborn Street—16 brown, stolid storeys with bay windows, built in 1891. Sullivan's legacy is the Auditorium building (built in 1889) and the Carson Pirie Scott Department Store (1899), both massive and ornately decorated. The Auditorium is now the campus of Roosevelt University, so you should pretend to be a student to examine its baroque interior.

While his contemporaries were getting excited about skyscrapers, Frank Lloyd Wright decided to go the opposite way—out to the suburbs. He reasoned that if the future of the workplace was going to lie in high-rises bunched together in the centre of cities, then the future of home life would lie in spacious refuges on the edge of town. And as it turned out, the merchant princes who were paying for the radical new workplaces wanted the spirit of innovation to carry over into their new homes. They were moving into suburbs such as Oak Park, so Wright had no shortage of clients when he set up his studio there after he fell out with Sullivan in 1893. Forest Avenue is still dotted with early examples of his work (his own home and studio are on the corner of Forest and Chicago Avenues).

Wright's greatest influence on the look of our suburbs came through concepts called the Prairie House and the Usonian House. Developed in the early 1900s, the Prairie style involves building low and wide so the house nestles into its environment. The roof is flat, and inside, most walls are eliminated so the centre of the house is a big open room around a hearth, because that was how Wright thought the ideal family should live. The colours and decorations (such as leadlight windows) should reflect the earth and the trees in which the house is set. By the second decade of this century, Prairie House madness had broken out across America—every domestic architect belonged to the school and every client wanted one. Chicago's best example is the Robie House, built by Wright in 1910. It's now a student administration office at the University of Chicago.

But Prairie Houses were expensive to build, needing clients who were rich as well as open-minded. Challenged in the 1930s to create a home for 'the ordinary American', Wright came up with the Usonian House (a play on USA and Utopia). Its base was a concrete slab, coloured a warm orange, that contained pipes for steam or hot water. This provided uniform heating in winter and as a bonus, kept pets off the furniture (because they preferred to lie on the floor). Like the Prairie House, it was open plan, with just a couple of brick interior walls to support the flat roof. Because the family would have no servants, Wright made the kitchen the centrepiece, so anyone preparing dinner could watch children and talk to guests. In 1937, the first Usonian House cost $5000 to build—about a year's salary for a middle-class person. According to Wright's biographer Alexander Boulton, the Usonian initiated a revolution in American home construction: 'the Wright designs, reinterpreted by the Levitt Construction Company, are the basis for nearly every post World War II housing development in the country'.

But the revolution in home-making begun by Wright happened outside Chicago. Inside Chicago, the office building continues to obsess the architects. The city's latest reincarnation of Louis Sullivan is Helmut Jahn. His Northwestern Atrium Center on West Madison Street is a 37-storey cascade of curves in glass and steel. His fragile, sweeping United Airlines terminal at O'Hare Airport disproves the conventional wisdom that modern airports are all the same. In 1983 he tackled the renovation of a 1930 limestone and marble tower called the Board of Trade building, doubling its size by adding a pyramid-shaped back half which echoes in green steel the art deco lavishness of the original.

And if you think all modern Chicago architecture

is phallic, look at Jahn's State of Illinois building, built in 1985. It is a case of thanks for the mammary—hemispherical and also transparent. If you walk inside and look up from the hollow interior, you can see through the floors and walls and even into the machinery that runs the escalators and elevators. Jahn took literally the concept of 'open government'. Since it's the headquarters of the state administration, Jahn thought the voters were entitled to see everything their representatives were doing. It sounds like a very Wright idea.

Wright himself went through a change of heart about the skyscraper. After initially condemning the soullessness of city high-rises, calling them the last gasp of discredited capitalism, Wright gradually let himself climb. In 1907 he reconstructed the interior of an 11-storey office block in central Chicago called The Rookery, originally built in 1888. The heavy exterior gives no hint of the delicate skylighted gold and marble courtyard Wright created inside. In 1936 he designed a beautiful open plan office building for the Johnson Wax company in Buffalo, New York. Then in 1951 he created a 19-storey office and apartment complex in Bartlesville, Oklahoma, for the Price Construction Company. Wright insisted that the building have no square corners because this was a waste of space and made special furniture for the triangular and parallelogram-shaped rooms.

At the time of his death in April 1959, construction was almost complete on his huge beehive-shaped Guggenheim Museum in New York. But Frank Lloyd Wright's biggest dream was destined never to be built. It was a project called Sky City on the Chicago lakeside. It had 528 storeys and would be four times the height of the Empire State Building, with the inhabitants delivered to their homes by helicopter or by atomic-powered lifts. The drawing he did of it in 1956 was seven metres long. The city planners took one look at the Sky City plan and dismissed it. There is a limit, even for Chicago.

4 · DOWN HOUSE, KENT, AND DORSET, ENGLAND

Karl Marx began writing *Das Kapital* while living with his wife and five children in a two-room flat above 28 Dean Street, London. He had published *The Communist Manifesto* in Brussels in 1848, but it had not exactly rocketed to the top of the bestseller lists, so by the time he moved to London in 1850, he was broke. For six years, Karl spent his days in the Reading Room of the British Museum, developing the case for public ownership of property, while Jenny Marx stayed home and tried to keep the children alive. Despite her efforts, three of them died of pneumonia. When one-year-old Franziska died in April 1852, the Marxes were too poor to afford a funeral. For three days the body stayed in bed while the living family members slept on the floor of the other room until they could borrow enough money for a coffin. Somehow during this period Karl found time to start an affair with

Lenchen, the maid who received no wages. She bore him a boy, who also lived in the flat.

If Karl Marx looked out of his window today he'd see the symptoms of a form of capitalism he could never have envisaged. Dean Street is Yuppie Central. It is lined with bars, clubs and cafes full of smoke and nattily dressed office workers. Just down the road, at number 44, is the Groucho club (named after another Marx who once said he would never belong to a club that would have him as a member). It buzzes with publishing and advertising types running up liquor bills.

There's a blue plaque on Karl's flat, noting the years he was there, but otherwise there is no physical sign of the family's period of residence, no atmosphere to conjure up Marx's spirit. The two rooms are a storage area for the Quo Vadis restaurant underneath. No entrepreneur has plans to refurnish the flat as it would have been in Marx's day. It's assumed that too few people would be willing to pay admission.

An insight into Marx's character more thought-provoking than those bare walls can be found in Down House in Kent, about an hour's journey south of Dean Street. Down House was for 40 years the home of Charles Darwin. It was where he proved through experimentation and logical analysis that human beings were not created on the sixth day in the image of God.

It's arguable whether Darwin's evolution or Marx's communism have become the most influential idea of the 20th century. I'd tend to give the prize to Charles, since his reputation is still growing, while Karl, through no fault of his own, is going through an unpopular phase. In any case, on a shelf in Darwin's study, next to a book called *Dogs: Their Points, Whims, Instincts &c*, I came upon a copy of *Das Kapital Volume 1*, with the words 'given to Charles

Darwin by Karl Marx 1873' engraved on the spine. Inside was a humble dedication to Darwin 'from his sincere admirer, Karl Marx'. Marx was 55 and unknown when he sent the book to Darwin, while Darwin was 64 and the most famous scientist in the world. His *On the Origin of Species by Means of Natural Selection* had been published in 1859, and *The Descent of Man* in 1871.

I asked the caretaker of Down House if there was any record of Darwin having actually read the copy of *Das Kapital* that Marx had sent him, and she said she didn't know. 'But he did write to Marx,' she said. 'Would you like to see the letter?' Darwin's letter turned out to be one small sheet. To me it suggests, very politely, that Darwin had no intention of reading the book, but Marx, who would have needed cheering up, may have read it otherwise. Darwin thanks Marx for sending the book, admits that he does not know much about political economy, and concludes: 'Though our lives have been so different, I believe that we both earnestly desire an extension of knowledge, and that this in the long run is all to the happiness of mankind'.

Did Darwinism or Marxism increase the happiness of mankind? Or did both of them increase our uncertainty and anger? Would we be better off if nobody had discovered alternatives to creationism and capitalism? Those are the questions I was pondering as I retraced Darwin's steps along the sand walk he constructed in his garden at the back of Down House.

Darwin used the sand walk to help him figure out the problems he had in explaining the animals he'd seen during his five-year voyage round the world as unpaid naturalist on a ship called *The Beagle*. The walk is an oval shape, about half a kilometre long, partly shaded by heavy foliage and partly in the sunshine. Each time Darwin made a circuit, accompanied by his fox terrier Polly, he would kick aside a pebble of flint at the end of the walk. An easy problem would mean a two-pebble walk and a tough one might mean a six-pebble marathon. You could say that the discovery of evolution depended on the flintstones.

It was at the end of one such thinking session, in 1844, that Darwin wrote to a friend: 'At last, gleams of light have come and I am almost convinced (quite contrary to the opinion I started with) that species are not (it is like confessing to murder) immutable'.

The garden also contains the large round stone on which Darwin observed the behaviour of the earthworms he was breeding. Inside the house you can see, jumbled together in dusty chaos, Darwin's microscopes, the hammers with which he chipped fossils out of rockfaces, his pistols and gunpowder, and the chair and board on which he wrote his books.

Charles Darwin was able to devote himself full-time to solving the riddle of evolution because his family connections with Wedgwood pottery kept him, his wife and his seven children comfortably cushioned from the poverty that plagued Karl Marx. And, as Marx would have noted, wealth begets wealth. Amongst the papers on display at Down House is a ledger sheet from 1881, the year before Darwin's death at the age of 73, in which he added up the earnings from the sales of his books. The total is £10,248. Even these days, such a figure would be a good income for an author, but in its time, it must have been a fortune.

Nevertheless, those who inherited Darwin's home allowed it to fall into ruin. I visited Down House at the end of 1995, when it was at its worst. The walls were spongy with damp, the woodwork in the greenhouse was rotten, the roof had fallen in on Darwin's laboratory. There was a serious risk it might close down forever. In 1996 it received a grant of £3 million from the fund created from the proceeds of Britain's national lottery and the curators began a renovation program. Of course, it is essential to preserve the place where humanity discovered its origins, to allow succeeding generations to take the walk that changed the world, but I suspect Darwin would have felt there was something very natural about letting his physical reminders fade and crumble, and Marx would tell us that the power of an idea will always outlive personal possessions.

At this point, this chapter should end. But if I moved on to E now, I would have failed to tell you about another essential place—the most English place in England, which also, as it happens, begins with D . . .

London is such a racial and cultural melting pot these days that you can easily forget how this large island off Europe was settled 1500 years ago by a bunch of sandy-haired, pink-cheeked Angles, Saxons and Danes. But three hours' drive southwest of London, their descendants inhabit farms and villages and pubs along a rugged coastline, still speak in the rolling dialect of Thomas Hardy novels and are willing to let travellers stay in the spare rooms of their houses and observe their folkways.

The region called Dorset is where everything in English history happened. Humour me for a moment and try this exercise: draw up a mental list of the main events in history that you may vaguely recall from your schooldays. If you're like me, you got a jumble that included the Roman invasion, King Canute and the Vikings, William the Conqueror, the Black Plague, Magna Carta, the war between the Cavaliers and the Round-heads, the Spanish Armada, Christopher Wren building

St Paul's Cathedral, and the madness of King George. Would you believe that all those events either started in Dorset or left a profound residue there? I'll convince you with the details later in this chapter.

And then there's all the stuff they didn't teach about Dorset at school. Ocean bathing was invented there. It's where T. E. Lawrence (of Arabia) fatally hit his head. The union movement started with a bunch of farm workers who held meetings in 1834 near the Dorset village of Tolpuddle. When they asked for higher pay they got sentenced to be transported to Australia. (The Tolpuddle Martyrs were later pardoned after a public protest campaign, but one of them didn't learn of his freedom for four years, because he was working on an outback sheep station.) Jane Austen, who became the hottest name in movies and television in the mid-90s, nominated Dorset as her favourite holiday spot, which raises the scary thought that Dorset could be the next Provence.

And of course Thomas Hardy wrote about Dorset. I've never met a person who voluntarily finished a Hardy novel, nor anyone who didn't find him melodramatic and tedious when forced to read him at school or university. So having told you that his house is just outside Dorchester and that there's a reconstruction of his study in the Dorset Museum, I won't need to mention him again.

Presumably this mixture of historical, literary and anthropological significance is what makes Dorset the place where foreign travel writers like to experience English hospitality and then complain about it. Bill Bryson, in his book *Notes from a Small Island*, hits the Dorset coastal path and engages in a 'dreary wet tramp along low hills above a pounding surf'. He finds a hotel that is 'a place of deep and depressing cheerlessness, with nylon sheets and cold radiators'. He goes to a pub in Lulworth and finds that it 'had that sickly stale smell of slopped beer and was full of flashing fruit machines. I was almost the only customer in the place but nearly every table was covered with empty pint glasses and ashtrays overflowing with fag ends, crisp packets and other disorderly detritus. My glass was sticky and the lager was warm'.

In a Lulworth restaurant Bryson finds mediocre food and service of 'resplendent ineptitude': 'Almost every dish that appeared from the kitchen had something on it that hadn't been ordered or lacked something that had . . . I ordered a prawn cocktail, waited thirty minutes for it, and then discovered that several of the prawns were frozen'.

I particularly enjoyed Bryson's portrait of a typical English guesthouse proprietor, not exclusive to Dorset, whom he calls Mrs Smegma. When Bryson arrives, she reels off a list of rules that must be obeyed by guests, including how to wipe their feet and use the toilet brush and when they can receive phone calls and use the bath. She concludes: 'Do be so good, would you, as to remove your counterpane each night. We've had some unfortunate occurrences with stains. If you do damage the counterpane, I will have to charge you'. When Mrs Smegma leaves the room, Bryson takes a pee in the sink and wonders: 'Just what the fuck is a counterpane?'

Paul Theroux, who is usually a bigger complainer than Bryson, remains curiously polite about Dorset in *The Kingdom By The Sea*, considering how depressing he found the rest of the English coastline. He just makes Dorset seem dull. Theroux labels Swanage 'the sort of half-asleep small town that was perfect after a long walk'. He thinks he could live in Weymouth because 'it was grand without being pompous . . . I liked the look of the houses, their elegance, and the smell of fish and beer'. He finds the deserted beach leading to Lyme Regis spooky: 'I expected to find a corpse, a murder victim, a suicide, or more likely someone who had accidentally drowned and been washed ashore'.

My first experience of Dorset was the exact opposite of Bryson's. I was with three other adults and a five-year-old boy spending a long weekend at a farm called Powerstock Mill in the western half of Dorset. The mill has been turning there for more than 1000 years and the house was built 200 years ago. These days the family takes in occasional boarders to supplement the farm income.

After we've put our bags upstairs in the rooms with the little porcelain jugs and saucers lined up along the beams, 10-year-old Edward Marsh, son of the owner, puts on his gumboots and takes us for a tour of the farm. Near the pond, we witness a vicious attack on Edward's dog by a little black duck. We pass the vegetable patch and see the beehives and the hens which make the honey and the eggs we'll be having for breakfast. Edward's dad waves to us as he leads the cows into the shed to produce the milk we'll have in our tea.

As we set off across the green fields, Edward warns us about stinging nettles, but points out that if we brush against one, we need only find a dock plant and rub its leaves on our skin to counteract the sting. Behind the Norman church we find a stone casket marked 'Here lieth the boddie of Roger Syme of West Minton who deceased the 4th of Iune ano dom 1657'. The front of the church is decorated with a stone figure wearing a crown. Edward answers our inquiry with: 'Oi don't know but oi think it moight be King Wenceslas'. Listening to Edward and other local speakers, I realise that many of the pronunciations we think of as Australian must have originated with immigrants from Dorset.

The Marshes ask if our young chap would like to have his dinner with Edward, so the adults can go and eat at the village pub. And so in the long summer twilight we walk to the Three Horseshoes Inn, which serves a sensational dinner on a terrace overlooking a stream and a hillside scattered with stone cottages. There's home-grown asparagus, a soup made with a local fish called gurnard, fried pigeon breasts with mushrooms, rack of Dorset lamb with garlic and rosemary, strawberry meringue and apricot compote with triple cream. Every ingredient comes from within 30 kilometres of Power-stock. I decide to take back all the generalisations I've ever made about English food (see Chapter 5). And the wine list is French.

The next day we join the Marshes for breakfast of porridge and fried eggs, sausages, bacon and tomato. We drive for half an hour to see the Cerne Giant, a 50-metre tall chalk figure scratched into a hillside, with a massive club and an erection to match. The theory is that it represents Hercules, and was put there 2000 years ago. The locals say that couples who are having trouble conceiving should sleep out on the giant's hillside overnight, and they'll be parents quick as a flash.

We take a long walk over the clifftops, past grazing sheep and cows and rabbits, and eat steak and kidney pie at a wreckers' and smugglers' pub called the Anchor Inn. We learn that local folk used to make a lot of money from salvaging the cargo of ships wrecked off the coastline, and they protested against the building of a lighthouse as an infringement on their livelihood. In the 18th century, Dorset was also a haven for smugglers bringing brandy, wine, silk, tea and escaped political prisoners from

France. (In January 1995 a package of cocaine valued at a million pounds was washed ashore near here, which suggests some traditions haven't died.)

Then we reach the sweet sad coastal town of Lyme Regis, stuck permanently in the 1920s, where the English still roll up their trousers and sit in deckchairs or in family-size bathing boxes on the grey slimy beach. Travellers willing to brave the wind can stroll to the end of the 14th century sea wall called The Cobb, which Louisa Musgrave jumped off in *Persuasion*, and where The French Lieutenant's Woman awaited her lover. The author of that novel, John Fowles, lives in Lyme and is curator of the local museum, which is full of fossils. We stroll past pink cottages with walls warped by age, and buy a bag of sticky toffees at the sweet shop, but we don't eat too many, because we're due back at Powerstock Mill Farm for tea and Mrs Marsh's fruit cake.

The only sour note in our three-day Dorset symphony is when one of our group is stung in the head by a bee while sitting in a deckchair in the Marshes' garden.

Convinced that Dorset is paradise, we decide to return two years later for a whole week. With an extra child in our party, we need a bit more space, so we book another farmhouse—or more accurately, a converted 18th century tithe barn. It's near Lulworth, at the opposite end of Dorset from our last experience and also, as it turns out, at the opposite end of the hospitality spectrum.

We've been told that although the owners live nearby, the establishment is 'self-catering', so we've brought towels and the makings of meals. On our arrival, we are confronted ('greeted' is not quite the word) by a tall gentleman with bushy eyebrows who proceeds to list the rules to be observed by guests. Children are not permitted to play in the 'prize-winning garden', nor to use the bedroom at the far end because their noise might disturb the owners (who, as it turns out, live underneath). Nor must children ride on the rocking horse, because it is 'part of the furnishings, not a plaything'. There is no phone but we can use a pay-phone downstairs. They will do our laundry for us with 24-hours' notice at a cost of £4.50 per machine load. If we are going out, all windows and doors must be fully secured. We must not drive at more than five miles per hour on the property. Strictly no chip pans or open-flame candles. Yes, we have fallen into the hands of Mr Smegma!

After our host concludes the briefing we find there is no soap in either bathroom and only one half-used roll of toilet paper. I go downstairs and ask if he could let us have some bathroom supplies. 'You were informed that this was self-catering,' he says. I point out that the local shops are now closed. He says he'll see what he can do, and an hour later appears with a single bar of soap and one toilet roll. As we study our accommodation we discover it is crammed with pretentious Victoriana that represents a yuppie's fantasy of Olde England—chamber pots, silver-plated goblets, leather-bound books, two broken sewing machines, and a cupboard full of Wedgwood china, which is locked.

The next day we try lunch at the Castle Inn at Lulworth Cove and realise it must be the place Bill Bryson was writing about. Its specialties are freshly defrosted crumbed scampi and grumpy service, which culminates in a waitress clearing our table in mid meal with the comment: 'Can I take these plates so we can get the washing up started?'

To cheer up the kids we pay four pounds each to enter a nearby attraction called Monkey World. It proves to be a collection of diseased chimpanzees who sit comatose in their cages or bang their heads against the bars. We learn that they have been 'rescued' from research laboratories who no longer need their services. Monkey World is trying to restore their sanity.

We decide that Dorset can only get better, and it does. We find a pub that actually cooks traditional Dorset food—the New Inn at Church Knowle. There's whole local trout, grilled, and a rich 'Blue Vinny Soup' containing a local form of gorgonzola cheese melted into chicken stock with celery, onion and herbs. The only manifestation of English hospitality as Bill Bryson encountered it is a large sign in the bar declaring: 'We do NOT serve portions of chips', but the chips that arrive with the trout are fat and delicious. They offer wines from Portugal, Hungary, South Africa and Corsica. Perhaps the smugglers brought them.

We absorb more Dorset atmosphere through the local paper—*The Swanage and Wareham Advertiser* ('14,880 copies each week'). It reports with alarm on page one that a loophole in council regulations could allow a sex shop to open in Dorset. On page three it laments that a folk-dancing group called the Old Harry Morris Men have decided to hang up their bells and call it a day. The group's leader says displays of Morris dancing are in great demand, but 'the paradox is that this demand has not encouraged new dancers to join our ranks. We need at least ten to remain viable and numbers have now slipped to six'.

And the paper announces that the Adult Education Sub-Committee of Dorset County Council has banned the teaching of tarot card reading from all adult education classes in Dorset. Councillor Ray Smith, a member of the sub-committee, explains: 'My personal opinion is that religion or politics shouldn't be in the adult education programme. It could attract some of these way out sects. Tarot is like ouija boards, you could get led in the wrong direction. I've had experience in the Far East countries and know of such things as voodoo'.

In the same local newsagency I pick up a booklet called *Folklore and Witchcraft in Dorset and Wiltshire.* It points out that on Shrove Tuesday children can go 'Lent-crocking' from house to house, singing: 'I be come a shroving For a little pancake, A bit o bread o your baking, Or a little truckle cheese of your making. If you'll gi me a little, I'll axe thee no more. If you don't gi me nothing I'll rattle your door'. On the Witches' Sabbath (October 31) you can peel an apple in one piece and throw it over your shoulder. On the floor it will reveal the initial of the person you are to marry.

The booklet continues: 'In Dorset the best way of keeping witches and fairies from your house, was to put in the chimney a bullock's head full of thorns, nails or pins'. This sounds like useful advice, because the booklet reports that 'a Dorchester lady claimed to have used her gifts in the summer of 1969 for a political purpose. Calling up the aid of Mr John Strachey, the War Minister, as her spirit guide, she cast a spell on Brigadier Woods, the Commandant of Bovington Camp. He was killed when his helicopter crashed. Not long ago, a Wimborne woman boasted that she had got rid of an unpleasant husband by bewitching him. Within three weeks, to the astonishment of his friends, he dropped down dead'. It's encouraging to see the old traditions have not entirely vanished.

I promised earlier to prove that Dorset is connected with everything you can remember about English history. Let us begin. There's a massive grass-covered fortress called Maiden Castle which was built by the Celts around

200 BC and overrun in 43 BC by the Romans under Vespasian (a future emperor on the way up). It's a monument to the obsolescence of military hardware. Archaeologists have found an ammunition dump of 20,000 beach pebbles stockpiled inside the fortress, waiting to be fired by state-of-the-art slingshots that had a range of 30 metres. The occupants of Maiden Castle never had a chance to use their ammunition. The Roman centurions arrived with the next generation of weaponry—a catapult called a ballista, which could hurl 20-kilogram weights more than 100 metres. Archaeologists have also dug up 34 skeletons from inside the ramparts of the fortress. All had bones showing injuries from ballista bolts.

King Canute began his invasion of England through the Dorset town of Wareham in 1015 (and supposedly died in nearby Shaftesbury Abbey). If he ever went to a beach and showed his worshipful courtiers that he couldn't stop the waves, it was probably Chesil Beach (which would also have been the source of the pebbles stockpiled by the Celts 1000 years earlier). The Normans drove the Vikings out, or settled them down, and in 1080 William the Conqueror started building Corfe Castle on top of a hill in eastern Dorset. King John (of Magna Carta fame) extended the castle and imprisoned French soldiers in its dungeons.

The Bubonic Plague came ashore in 1348, carried by fleas on rats leaving a ship moored in the Dorset port of Melcombe, near Weymouth. The Black Death killed a third of Britain's population. Barely had the Dorset folk recovered than they were in the thick of the civil war. Corfe Castle was a royalist stronghold besieged by the forces of parliament, who blew up most of it for revenge after the Cavaliers had emerged. The modern ruins are so massive you realise they must have used the equivalent of an atom bomb.

The Spanish Armada fought the English navy just off Lyme Bay, providing plenty of salvage for the local wreckers. Christopher Wren quarried 60,000 tons of stone from the island of Portland, adjoining Weymouth, to build St Paul's Cathedral, and was the member of parliament for Weymouth in 1702.

To recover from the porphyria which caused his madness, King George III took regular holidays at Weymouth, turning it into Britain's most fashionable resort in the 1790s. He is credited with popularising ocean bathing. You can still swim at the pebbly beach where George's servants wheeled his bathing box into the water while a band hidden in another bathing box struck up *God Save The King*. But take note of a medical pamphlet called *Observations on Sea Bathing*, issued at the time by 'J.C. Residing Phyfician at Weymouth', which advises: 'The moft proper Time of Bathing is early in the Morning; before which no exercife ought to be taken; all previous Fatigue tending to diminifh that Force which the Fibres when contracted will otherwife have, of removing Obftructions more effectually . . . To Bathe late in the day (more efpecially in hot Weather) will occasion great Depreffion of the Spirits, particularly in debilitated or paralytic Perfons'.

Dorset's most famous 20th century resident was Thomas Edward Lawrence. An archaeologist by training, Lawrence persuaded the Arabs to help the British in World War I but got disgusted when the British sold out the Arabs afterwards. In the late 1920s he enlisted in the British air force under the name of Shaw, and ended up at Bovington military camp in Dorset. He bought a cottage called Cloud's Hill near the camp and lived there until 13 May 1935, when he was riding his motorcycle towards the cottage with a lamb chop in his knapsack to cook for lunch (by his open fire since he had neither gas nor electricity in his spartan home). The official version says that he was going too fast, swerved to avoid two boys on bicycles, lost control of the bike, crashed and died. But if you visit Cloud's Hill you'll encounter a caretaker who raises the question of a big black car that was passing at the time and was never identified. If Lawrence was planning some new denunciation of British foreign policy, working secretly for the Government, or still dealing with factions in the Arab world, his death may not have been accidental.

Over the doorway of his cottage Lawrence had engraved a Greek slogan that loosely translates as 'What Me Worry', which he said 'means that nothing in Cloud's Hill is to be a care upon its inhabitant. While I have it there shall be nothing exquisite or unique in it. Nothing to anchor me'. In fact, he cluttered the cottage with photos, drawings and books, any of which might offer a clue to his murder. The caretaker will discuss them with you at more length than you may desire.

You don't need to know any of that to have a fine time in Britain's answer to Provence, or to study the English at their most English, but the knowledge that you are where all of English history happened may prove some consolation if you find yourself staying with the Smegmas.

5 · EATING PLACES

Of all the motives for travelling, the quest for the great meal seems to me the most admirable. That's because it is not just about food. It's about understanding other cultures through the ways they choose to sustain themselves. Eating is, after all, the most important thing that humans do; without it, they can do nothing else.

When I talk about the quest for the great meal, I do not mean the expensive meal. The priciest joints are usually the least revealing of the real life of a country. A great meal may not even taste particularly fine by your usual standards, but it will be great if it teaches you a new way of judging.

For travellers who like to eat, or to watch how others eat, the world can be divided into two types of nation: the Spontaneous Countries and the Planning Countries. A Spontaneous Country is one where you can walk into just about any restaurant or cafe and be pretty confident of an interesting meal. Because the locals value good food, the average cook tends to be dedicated, skilful and eager to please, and travellers become the incidental beneficiaries of a national tradition. Models of Spontaneous Countries are Italy, France and Thailand.

Then there are lands where the general expectation of cooking is so low that an interesting meal can only be assured by doing vast amounts of homework beforehand, studying and cross-indexing guidebooks and advice from other travellers. Examples of Planning Countries are Britain, America and all of Eastern Europe. Australia is currently in the process of changing from a Planning Country to a Spontaneous Country. The serious gastronaut can find good food in these places, but it's likely to be much more expensive than good food in Spontaneous Countries.

Here are some observations on eating places which have been revelations to me—places that are, if not always essential, at least worth a pilgrimage if you find yourself within 500 kilometres. Let's begin with the Spontaneous Countries, which still often contain pockets that require planning.

In spontaneous countries

Florence

Considering that it's the artistic capital of the most food-conscious nation on earth, Florence has a lot of rotten restaurants. Tourism has created cynicism. I'd be inclined to use Florence only for its museums and to eat out of town. But if you're stuck in Florence at lunchtime, you'll find one oasis: Cibreo. It's located well away from the crowds near the Sant'Ambroglio market.

The restaurant's name refers to an old aristocratic dish of cockscombs, giblets and livers served with egg yolks and lemon juice. You may be relieved that Cibreo doesn't actually serve this treat any more, especially since there's no menu, and you're expected to eat whatever they suggest that day. (There's no wine list either—just choose a bottle from the shelves.) They'll usually start with a soup—I got a creamy yellow capsicum puree with an intensity of flavour I've never been able to replicate. Then you might receive duck stuffed with pinenuts and raisins, or lamb stuffed with artichokes, followed by bitter chocolate tart with pears. Cibreo's owners are aware of their uniqueness in Florence, so you could end up paying a significant sum for the full experience.

Hong Kong

It would be difficult to have a bad meal in Hong Kong, but it's easy to find waiters who answer 'You no like' when you ask them to explain something written in Chinese on a menu. You end up suspecting the Chinese customers are eating much more interestingly than you are. The solution is to visit places that require no language.

Head for a part of Kowloon called Lei Yue Mun, which is basically a vast open-air market for living seafood. Point at the tanks containing the fish, prawn, lobster, clam or nameless creature that takes your fancy, haggle over the price if you enjoy that sort of thing, and then carry your purchase upstairs to one of the restaurants that operate on a BYO-food principle. Let them decide what form of spicing and slicing and cooking will best suit the creature, and soon they'll deliver a steaming banquet.

For lighter moods, you could visit a place which serves *dim sum*—tasty tidbits that are wheeled past on trolleys, enabling you to point at the ones you want. (Note that I don't use the term *yum cha*, which literally means 'take tea', for this type of meal, because in Hong Kong that is regarded as a lower-class way to describe a refined ritual.)

The most historic of the Hong Kong dim sum places is the Luk Yu teahouse, which has been serving tidbits to gentlefolk since 1925. A visit to Luk Yu is as essential as taking a ride on the Star Ferry. When it had to move premises in 1975, Luk Yu brought along all its fittings, so you still climb creaking wooden stairs to eat under revolving fans in polished wooden booths behind lacquered screens with spittoons on the floor. Some of the waiters look as if they've been there as long as the fittings.

First you should order your tea, and if you want something stronger than you ever imagined could exist, try the one called Iron Goddess of Mercy. You might then choose from the passing trolleys and trays, but you may still suspect that the Chinese are eating better than you, because there is also a bunch of 'specialty beautiful tidbits' listed on a sheet of paper that is printed only in Chinese. To order the specialties, you're expected to put a circle above the items you want. Do not be defeated by the pictograms. On page 54, I've reproduced the sheet I got, and numbered the items from right to left, as the Chinese would read them. The top half lists the savouries, the bottom right lists rice and noodle dishes, and the bottom left lists the desserts. Take this book with you when you go to Luk Yu, and you'll know as much as the Chinese customers.

1. Dumpling in special soup.
2. Steamed savoury rice in lotus leaves.
3. Sticky rice with mushroom.
4. Steamed heart of bamboo with minced shrimp.
5. Steamed bun with flavoured meats.
6. Crab meat with chives.
7. Tender pigeon with special sauce.

8. Country-style steamed dumpling.
9. Seafood dumpling.
10. Steamed prawn dumpling.
11. Oyster sauce barbecue bun.
12. Tender chicken large steamed bun.
13. Fried dumpling in soup.
14. High-class ham with minced fish in rolls.
15. Shredded chicken pancake.
16. Spring rolls with prawn and chives.
17. Barbecue pork with cod slices.
18. Pigeon meat on toast.
19. Beef dumplings.
20. Minced pork and liver dumplings.
21. Spare ribs steamed in special sauce.
22. Shark fin in special soup.
23. Mushroom and crabmeat mixed with noodles.
24. Prawn dumpling in special soup.
25. Fatty chicken baked rice.
26. Baked rice with pig tongue and fruity sauce.
27. Baked rice with sweet corn and diced cod.
28. Lotus paste in sticky rice wrapped in lotus leaf.
29. Egg yolk walnut paste bun.
30. Black sesame cream cake.
31. Red bean paste rolls.
32. Steamed bun in lard.
33. Tapioca in coconut milk.
34. Sweet omelette.
35. Sesame paste fried dumpling.
36. Custard-filled fried bun.
37. Lotus paste fried pancake.
38. Savoury sweet soup.
39. Shredded coconut tart.
40. Custard tart.
41. Orange juice custard tart.

新界美景茶樓

星期三　美點

新式美點應時供應　每日上午九時至下午九時
（服務費加一）

鹹品

1　上角
2　紗葉飯
3　荷葉飯
4　百花鷄盒
5　北菇鷄盒
6　竹笙蒸飯
7　鹵肉韮菜餃
8　乳豬
9　柱侯牛腩
10　淡水鮮蝦餃
11　蠔油叉燒飽
12　蟹黃鷄球大飽
13　煎粉菓
14　雲腿鯪魚班戟
15　鷄絲煎班戟
16　韮王蝦春卷
17　石燒燒賣
18　石燒叉燒飽
19　鮮牛肉燒賣
20　釀豬腸粉
21　柱侯蒸肉排

食小麵飯（飯麵小食）

22　紅燒大包
23　上湯水餃
24　上湯肉蝦
25　肥雞飯
26　焗豬扒飯
27　焗班肉粒飯

甜品

28　蓮子蓉香飽
29　合桃蓉香糕
30　黑芝蔴糊
31　紅豆沙
32　奶皮
33　椰汁西米露
34　黃梅煎堆
35　蔴蓉香酥炸
36　奶黃酥
37　蓮子蓉燒餅
38　甘露蘆兜甫
39　椰絲酥
40　油雲蛋
41　鮮橙汁

91 (33) 6000

If comparing these translations with the list seems a bit laborious, you could simply put circles above items at random, and look forward to whatever arrives.

Lausanne

Switzerland is a Spontaneous Country only for the rich, who can confine themselves to French-style restaurants and pay a lot for the privilege. Those on a budget will need to become connoisseurs of sausages and fondue. Somewhere between these extremes is La Grappe d'Or. It also offers a case study in community relations. It's in Lausanne, which is in the French-speaking part of Switzerland, although its chef is a German-speaker, which means he has a hard time persuading the locals that he can do anything more than stodge. The general assumption seems to be: the German Swiss make money, the Italian Swiss make love, and the French Swiss make meals. (The fourth linguistic group—the 50,000 Romansh speakers who live in the southeastern mountains—make too little noise to be stereotyped.)

The night of my visit to La Grappe d'Or was pretty quiet, so the kitchen started sending out extra dishes at random. The restaurant echoed with cries of 'I didn't order this' and the soothing voices of waiters explaining that the chef just thought the guests might like to try something new. It became apparent that my order of venison with chestnuts, red cabbage and *spaetzle* (little dumplings) had been too conservative, because my bonus plates included zucchini flowers stuffed with fish in a tomato broth, slices of marinated bream, and two baby lobsters sitting on a potato puree splashed with truffle-infused olive oil. The chef certainly convinced me that he could equal anything a French-speaker might create (at half the price), but I suspect the Lausannois might be harder to win over.

Madrid

After 9 p.m., you can't do better than to join the Madrilenos on the tapa trail, in search of tiny tastes displayed in smoky bars throughout the inner city. *Tapas*, the snack food of a nation, literally means 'lids', and refers to saucers of food that were originally served on top of wine glasses. The fun is in finding your own favourites, but as a starting point you could plunge into the labyrinth of lanes behind the police headquarters in Puerto del Sol (the spot from which all distances in Spain are measured). You might head for Casa Alberto at the end of Calle del Principe, where Cervantes lived (and presumably ate tapas) in 1614. Be prepared to wander into any open doorways along the way.

Walk up to the bar, order a glass of wine or sherry, and point to the foods you fancy from the array in front of you. Don't have too many tapas in any one bar, because there's always something new around the corner. Balance your diet with garlic potatoes in one place, barbecued octopus in another, sausages poached in cider here, pastries filled with tuna and peas there, and save room for the mussels whose shells you toss into a long trough at your feet. When you're staggering around stuffed and tipsy at 1am, the best stomach settler is a cup of hot chocolate into which you dip *churros* (fried sweet dough) from a street stall.

If you're in Madrid on a weekend, then you should hire a car and join the morning exodus to nearby Segovia, where foodies argue over the best places to taste roast lamb or suckling pig. The chef who roasts the beasts is called the *asador*, and all Spanish gourmets can detail the particular subtleties of their favourite asador. Madrilenos who want to combine a grand eating experience with a jaunt in the countryside look for an asador in one of the villages just outside Segovia, such as Torre Caballeros, where I found the best lamb I've ever eaten.

The procedure is to pass by your chosen restaurant about 11 a.m. and specify what you want, so the asador can put it in the oven to be ready by 1 p.m. Some restaurants let you choose your own live lamb from a flock gambolling in a nearby field, but you must allow extra time for them to slaughter it. I decided I was not quite at that level of connoisseurship, and simply asked for roast lamb, medium, at an antique wood-beamed place called Posada de Javier. Then my companions and I went for a long walk.

At lunchtime, we started with a dish of big white beans in pork gravy with slices of chorizo sausage, and a stew of wild asparagus and mushrooms. Then a fat man in a white apron thrust a shovel into a beehive oven and pulled out our haunch, which was sitting in an intense stock of white wine and herbs. With a local red wine called Tinto Pesquera, it was a perfect moment.

Paris

Call me a sucker for nostalgia, but La Coupole in Montparnasse charms me every time. Okay, it plays up its heritage as a bohemian eating hall where artists used to present paintings when they couldn't pay for meals, and okay, it now sells souvenir cups and ashtrays. But the night I found myself sitting next to a table of prostitutes on their dinner break, being entertained by their cigar-sucking pimp, I decided that La Coupole is still the real Paris. Most of the customers order tall wire structures layered with oysters and crustaceans, which they rinse down with acidic white wines. I preferred the fatty cassoulet of goose with little beans and slices of peppery sausage. So did the hookers, I noticed. But they had the excuse of having to go back onto the chilly streets.

Paris has several restaurants which have been awarded three stars, the ultimate accolade of the red Michelin guide. The Michelin would argue that this makes them the finest restaurants in the world. I'd say it depends on whether you value spontaneity or predictability in your chef. Since Michelin's three-star rating depends as much on having crystal glasses and marble bathrooms as it does on food and service, it tends to encourage high prices and stuffy atmospheres, and to discourage innovation. The food becomes fossilised, the service becomes arrogant. The only three-star restaurant in Madrid, for example, is Zalacain, which offers old-fashioned French dishes or Spanish dishes that have been fussed and flounced to appeal to conservative French tastes. You eat more enjoyably in any tapas bar. In London, Michelin awards three stars to Le Gavroche, an obscenely expensive place that requires gents to wear ties and which was downgraded by Britain's *Good Food Guide* for allowing cigar smoking during dinner.

If you have a few hundred dollars left over in your travel budget, Paris is the place to compare Michelin's criteria with your own. My case study is La Tour d'Argent, which has existed in various Paris locations since 1582 and has had three stars since the Michelin started awarding them in the 1950s. In an earlier book called *The Obsessive Traveller*, I ventured the theory that La Tour d'Argent was one of the four best restaurants in the world. I had eaten there in the mid-1980s, and I remembered its view of the Seine and Notre Dame Cathedral, its warm intelligent service, its speciality of duck done 20 different ways, and being able to walk over and watch the chefs pressing your duck in a little theatre set up in the back of the dining room.

So when I decided to get married in Paris in 1991, I took my own advice and made a dinner booking at La Tour d'Argent for our wedding day. We were celebrating the event by staying for three nights at the Ritz Hotel (see Chapter 18) where you are supposed to ask the concierge to arrange your slightest whim. I asked if he would phone La Tour d'Argent and tell them it was our wedding day, and see if they could serve us a small cake to mark the occasion.

We were welcomed downstairs, shown to the little lift, welcomed again upstairs and shown to a window table with the view as I remembered it. We were hoping to eat some of the seasonal vegetables we'd seen in the Paris markets, but being a three-star restaurant, La Tour d'Argent doesn't go in for that sort of thing. The nearest we could find to a seasonal dish was chanterelle mushrooms served with foie gras (not pâté, the whole liver). And, of course, we ordered the house speciality—duck with a sauce made from its blood and liver plus cognac.

My wife doesn't drink red wine, so we asked the sommelier to recommend a white that would suit our meal. He turned the pages of the wine list to the red section and pointed to two light reds. No, we said, we would like a white. 'But it is impossible, sir,' he said. 'One drinks red wine with duck.' Surely, we said, in a list of more than 100 French white wines, there must be something that could be consumed with duck. 'Not really,' he said. 'You must try to have a red.' I ordered a chardonnay I had heard of called Puligny Montrachet. He shrugged and went away. It turned out to be sensational.

We'd enjoyed our entrée and were waiting to be told when to walk over and see our duck being pressed when the duck, already plated, arrived at the table. On busy nights, it seems, the staff don't have time to demonstrate the theatre. The duck was as fine as I remembered. Then came the wedding cake—in fact, a small rectangle of chocolate cake with two candles in it. The waiter said 'Happy birthday' as he delivered it. We decided it would be pointless to correct him.

The experience cost about $400. As we were leaving, we asked if we could take a copy of the menu as a souvenir, and were told that we could buy one in the gift shop. The shop (an inevitable part of all three-star restaurants these days) was crowded, even at 11 p.m., with Japanese tourists. It offered ties, scarves, ashtrays, umbrellas, cookbooks, placemats and towels, all bearing the Tour d'Argent insignia. We bought a menu, which was on silver-coated cardboard.

Two years later Michelin downgraded La Tour d'Argent from three stars to two. There is some justice.

Rome

Italians and Jews share a tradition of taking their nourishment seriously, and when you put them together you get Piperno, a dark wood-panelled shrine founded 160 years ago in a tiny square called Monte de Cenci, on the edge of Rome's ghetto. Subtle is not the word here. In the spring the speciality is *carciofi alla giuda*, young artichokes which are deep-fried in olive oil so they turn dark brown and crunchy. The menu reveals that in 1825 a Roman physiologist said artichokes 'make people perspire, and purify the blood, but they arouse unduly the passionate desire of the unmarried'. If that worries you, try the fried zucchini flowers, or the battered *bacala* (salt cod) or the gnocchi made with semolina flour and eggs instead of potato. In summer, Piperno displays an array of seafood that tends to defy the notion that the Mediterranean is fished out.

My particular fondness for Piperno arises from the way the waiters welcomed my three-year-old daughter, sat her on a cushion so she could see the whole table, gave her a tour of the kitchen and cut up her tagliatelle when they served it. But then, encouragement of children is another tradition shared by Jews and Italians.

Travellers who want to experience both the diversity of Italy's wines and the diversity of organs inside farm animals should head for a restaurant called Checchino (pronounced kekino). It's inside a cave dug into the side of a hill called Monte Testaccio, which was the rubbish dump of ancient Rome. The boats bringing oil up the Tiber used to throw their broken pots onto the hill, so that its sides are still studded with shards of pottery.

Having examined what must be the largest wine list in Italy, and settled on a fabulous red called Tignanello, I was intrigued to find on the menu a dish called *rigatoni alla pajata*. The letter *j* is not supposed to exist in the Italian alphabet (along with the letter *k*, which is rendered *ch* in Italian spelling) but there it was, in what I assumed to be a dialect word. In Spontaneous Countries I have a policy of ordering any dish I don't understand, because this usually leads to a discovery. All I could guess about this one was that it probably involved meat, because Checchino is opposite Rome's oldest slaughterhouse and specialises in the parts of animals other restaurants don't reach.

My Italian was as good as the waiter's English, so we were not up to solving the puzzle of how the letter *j* found its way into an Italian word. To explain *pajata* (pronounced pay-ah-ta), he drew a picture of a cow with an arrow pointing to its nether regions. Cow's bum? Cow's udder? Or some sophisticated internal organ? The dish turned out to be pasta cylinders in a light tomato sauce, with what looked like a shrivelled grey doughnut on top. The doughnut was rubbery and filled with something like sour ricotta cheese.

A few days later, in conversation with an Italian whose English vocabulary included animal anatomy, I learned that pajata is a Roman dialect word for the intestine of a calf that has not yet tasted grass. Everything else we ate at Checchino was superb. But from now on I'll take the appearance of the letter *j* in any Italian food word as a warning that there are some dishes Anglos are just not meant to eat.

Venice

The standard of food in Venice is the worst in Italy (which means it's still better than most cities outside the country). Perhaps the Venetian restaurateurs' contempt for their customers is not surprising after a 500-year tourist battering. What *is* surprising is that just across the bridge to the mainland, in the much maligned industrial town of Mestre, there's a great restaurant well known to Venetians and unknown to tourists. It's Trattoria dall'Amelia—one big wood-lined room divided by cupboards full of olive oil bottles, with poinsettias in flowerpots along the windowsills. Big central tables groan with bowls of weird-shaped shellfish and baskets of salad leaves of various shapes, sizes, and intensities of green. The customers are businessmen in dark suits and big family groups.

We heard no English spoken, except to us, by waiters who happily spent as long as we needed explaining dishes and recommending wines. If you order *cicheti veneziana*, you'll get a cold mixture of crumbed mussels, prawns, scallops, fish marinated in tomato sauce, and sea slugs. If you order *cicheti caldi* you'll get warm shrimp, corkscrew-shaped shellfish, snails and *bacala* (a puree of salt cod). We ordered both, of course, as well as artichoke gnocchi and the house speciality—tiny squid in a rich sauce of their own ink, with porridgey polenta.

The residents of Mestre are accused of destroying the beauty of Venice with the pollution from their factories. Trattoria dall'Amelia makes me inclined to forgive them.

In planning countries

Cairo

The eating habits of Egypt are best observed during the festival of Ramadan in early June, when the days are relatively cool and every night is a party. To honour the time when Mohammed received his revelations from God, Muslims are forbidden to eat, drink, smoke or have sex between sunrise and sunset. If you take a stroll through Cairo's old town around 6.30pm you'll see people with forks poised, sitting at long benches set up on the footpath. The benches are crammed with cigarette packets and bowls of bean stew. When the cannon goes off, signifying sunset, the people start shovelling and smoking, and when the meal is finished, they take to the streets—singing, dancing and riding on temporary merry-go-rounds that seem to have sprung up just for the occasion. Presumably the few people who stay indoors are having sex.

Health authorities warn that Ramadan is a period when sugar consumption soars and Egyptians put on weight, because the night-time meals—at 6.30, midnight and 3am, are far more lavish than their daytime equivalents the rest of the year. For your own sustenance, you could join the throngs at the street tables, or play it safe at a pleasant restaurant called Arabesque, in the middle of town not far from Midan el Tahrir (Liberation Square), or Garden Groppi, a cafe partly situated outdoors that became a legend with British soldiers in World War II.

When you tire of walking and dancing and having your hand shaken by beaming locals who say 'Welcome to my country' (and amazingly, they are not trying to sell you anything) you could collapse on a cushion in the world's oldest cafe. Fashawi's, in a narrow alley near the Kahn al-Khalili bazaar, has been a place of political plotting for 2000 years. Last century the French spies in Cairo nicknamed it Cafe des Mirroirs, not so much for its shiny surfaces but for the distorted reflections of reality they found there. More recently the fundamentalists who assassinated Anwar Sadat held their meetings at Fashawi's. You can order a pot of mint tea or a water pipe for a dollar or two (more if the pipe contains hash rather than tobacco). And don't worry if you happen to doze off on one of the frayed sofas. Around 3am, the official drum-bangers will be passing the door reminding everyone to catch those last precious bites before sunrise.

London

The current fad in London is for enormous restaurants—Quaglino's, for example, can seat 400 people in mirrored splendour and Mezzo can seat 700 people in three dining areas. They tend to be owned by the furniture shop millionaire Terence Conran, to be sumptuously decorated, to have waiters better dressed than the customers, to serve a mixture of Italian and French bistro food with the occasional Asian touch, and to employ a lot of Australian cooks, because this sort of food has been standard fare in Sydney for nearly a decade.

These caverns may be worth visiting to observe London yuppies at play, but if your priority is eating well, then Bibendum is better. Bibendum was the tyre man that symbolised the Michelin company, so his bulbous form appears often in the decor of the restaurant that bears his name in the former tyre factory in South Kensington. He's in the ashtrays, the carafes, the leadlight windows, even round the table legs. Children of a certain age will wonder if the restaurant is dedicated to the Mutant Ninja Turtles.

Bibendum ain't cheap, but there's a generosity in the servings and a heartiness in the flavourings that dispels the fear that you've entered a temple of nouvelle cuisine. My memory locks onto a plate of sliced cotechino sausage and veal kidneys with lentils and mustard sauce, and a roasted rabbit with a stew of eggplant and capsicums. The desserts of intense blackcurrant jelly and poached nectarines came with heavy Jersey cream, which is one English cooking tradition I'm glad Bibendum has retained.

Los Angeles

So you think Mexican food looks and tastes like something that somebody already ate? A small wooden restaurant called La Serenata di Garibaldi will change your mind. It defies the faddishness of Los Angeles because its intended clientele is not the Hollywood crowd but the local Mexican community (who turn around and stare when a gringo comes in). It is most unfashionably positioned at 1842 East First Street, Downtown. To reach it, you drive down a trash-filled alley and into a small carpark, then clamber up a fire escape and through a screen door, which is when the smells hit you.

Don't order starters because the table will be quickly

covered with *quesadillas* (small cheese pancakes), and bowls of pumpkin soup and corn chips with spicy dips. Then you'll need the waiter's help in choosing among main courses. One house speciality is called *por si no te vuelvo a ver* (if I read my sauce-stained notes correctly). This translates as 'if I never see you again', which falls somewhat short of revealing that it is a dish of spicy rice and broccoli with barbecued scallops, clams and shrimp. Then there's roast chicken covered with a *pipian* puree of pumpkin seeds and peppers, or shrimp in a sauce of chipotle chillies, or *mahi mahi* (a meaty fish) in mustard sauce. Dessert should be a soothing caramel flan.

New York

Rich Manhattanites like to punish themselves by eating in overpriced restaurants with dull food and snobby service, such as The Four Seasons. The few who are free of guilt go to Le Cirque, which offers helpful service, refined French-Italian food, and the chance to observe the power elite at play. Unlike The Four Seasons, where you'll be banished to a back room (known as Siberia), while those approved by the head waiter dine in an area known as Paradise, Le Cirque is small enough to put a stranger such as you at a table next to Henry Kissinger.

But if your budget won't let you indulge your curiosity about the manners of the rich, take the subway towards the bottom of the island and try The Savoy, a homely place in Soho with flowerpots in the window, battered cutlery, cracked plates and fascinating food. Every nation on earth has contributed to the menu—garlic soup, pappardelle with morel mushrooms and almond gremolata, red snapper with shrimp and beans, bread-and-butter pudding—and the details are done so lovingly that all your prejudices about the horrors of The Big Apple melt rapidly away.

Prague

Prague is a wonderful city, to which I would return at the slightest provocation, but next time I'll take fibre supplements and vitamin tablets. Dried out duck and claggy dumplings are the high points of the local cuisine, plus occasional cabbage. Constipation sets in after three days. At a much vaunted restaurant called U Pavouka (at the spider), which has an accordionist, I was relieved to discover a dish translated as 'vegetable risotto'. It proved to be two mounds of white rice and a mound of diced carrots, corn and peas, obviously from a tin, and totally flavourless.

If you don't mind paying Paris prices, the best restaurant in town is U Modre Kachničky (at the Blue Duckling), which doesn't mind you knowing that the Rolling Stones, Meryl Streep and Vaclav Havel have eaten there before you, and which specialises in venison goulash with dumplings, duck with apples and honey, and rabbit in cream sauce with mushrooms. The best low-priced meal I had in Prague was a chewy sausage with mustard on a piece of rye bread, bought from a stall in Wenceslas Square. When I asked what was in the sausage, I was told 'pig tumours', which may have lost something in translation.

Seattle

Imagine, if you will, that someone has decided to stuff a small elephant into a purse. They've done a reasonable sort of job, with just a couple of bulges here and there, but they've been defeated by the trunk, which protrudes for about half a metre out one side. Now you have a mental picture of a geoduck, one of the delicacies of Seattle, in the northwest of the USA. Geoduck (a kind of mutated clam with a tube attached) is pronounced gooeyduck, for reasons not apparent. You can see a wide selection of them pulsating obscenely on stalls in Seattle's Pike Place market. They are part of the reason Seattle is now regularly described as the foodie capital of America.

Seattle is on one of the last unpolluted waterways in the developed world; it enjoys access to a spectacular range of fish and crustaceans and edible seaweeds. It gets rain nine months of the year (or *only* nine months of the year, as the locals say), so fruits and vegetables just spring out of the ground.

It's also surrounded by mountains and forests, in which grow multitudes of mushrooms, with names like portabella, king boletus, oak log-grown shiitake, and crimini trentini ('excellent for stuffing' says the sign on the market stall). The forests yield game birds, venison and wild fruits such as cloudberry and huckleberry. The rivers spawn five species of salmon, served fresh, marinated, dried or smoked, in such quantities that many Seattlites hope never to see another salmon in their lives. Seattle is an example of a Spontaneous City in a Planning Country.

My best meal there was at Chau's, a Chinese restaurant where cooking methods tested over centuries bring out the best in the live seafood—including eels and turtles—kept in tanks around the walls. I even got to try the dreaded geoduck, in hot garlic sauce with peppers. Apparently Chinese connoisseurs value geoduck more for its texture (crunchy rubber) than its flavour (mildly mussel).

Seattle is also known throughout America for its

obsession with coffee. Espresso bars and licensed coffee carts have proliferated through its suburbs over the past decade. The true Seattlite, I was told, drinks five or six cups of coffee a day and applies intense analysis to the process. It's important, first of all, to know who roasted the beans. There are four major roasters in Seattle, and the locals claim to be able to tell the difference, particularly in the degree to which the roasters have plucked out the burned beans. Cafes and carts display little signs indicating whether the beans were roasted by SBC (Stewart Brothers, who opened the city's first espresso bar in 1981), Starbucks (which spread the craze by opening a string of espresso bars in 1983), Torrefazione or Mauro (both founded in 1986). No wonder they called the movie *Sleepless in Seattle.*

Once you've found your roast, you must specify the way the coffee is to be served. Most fashionable at the moment is caffe latte—espresso topped up with steamed milk. (The locals claim that Seattle is an anagram of lattes, conveniently ignoring one *e*). But do you want the espresso diluted with water before the milk goes in? This is called an Americano. Do you want non-fat milk, low-fat milk, or half-milk half-cream? Do you want it tall (in a long cup with extra milk)? Do you want froth on the top? Do you want flavoured syrup added?

To save prolonged interrogations at the coffee cart, Seattlites have developed a coffee shorthand. Ask for 'a double tall skinny foamless almond' and you'll get a double-strength espresso in a long mug with low-fat milk, no froth and a little almond syrup. Ask for 'a Yankee dog with a white hat on a leash', and you'll get an Americano with froth, to take away. A decaff with non-fat milk is called a 'why bother'.

Confronted with these bewildering options, a traveller

is likely to ask for a cup of tea. Sorry, you'll have to make decisions about that too. At a restaurant called Ponti's Seafood Grill, the menu lists 20 'premium, first-pickings, tender, whole-leaf, loose teas'. If you're not prepared to be a connoisseur in all things, stay away from Seattle.

Vienna

After my vegetable-free experience of Prague, I was relieved to move on to Vienna, assuming in my innocence that it would offer culinary diversity. Certainly the restaurants in Austria are far more expensive than those in the Czech Republic, but the Viennese seem content to subsist on a diet of red meat and cream cakes.

A typical day might begin with coffee at Cafe Centrale, a vast chandeliered space under Moorish arches where Lenin and Trotsky used to plot socialism while earning their living as professional chess players. One of their contemporaries still sits at a table by the door— a bald, walrus-moustached poet named Peter Altenberg, reading a newspaper. On closer inspection, he proves to be a fibreglass sculpture. Altenberg rarely paid his bills while he was alive, so the cafe is getting some value out of him as decoration now he's dead. These days, of course, the Viennese in Cafe Centrale don't play chess or write poetry—they talk on their mobile phones.

Choose your newspaper on a stick from the rack, your cream cake from the glass case (for me, Esterhazy, which is chocolate and ground almonds, or Marillenkuchen, poppy and apricot), and your coffee from the 20 variations on the menu (Schlagobers is with whipped cream, Kaisermelange is with an egg yolk and brandy), then sit for two hours. Now you are ready to stroll to lunch. On a fine day you might sit in front of a dark brown restaurant called Zum Scherer on Judenplatz and try to reconcile the menu with your German dictionary. German is a language that loves compound words, so let me give just one example: *Fiakerschweinsmedaillons Bier-kummelsauce, Knoblauch Speckkartoffeln* is pork with a sauce of beer and caraway seeds and potatoes with garlic and bacon. A stroll through the cobbled streets is acceptable before your afternoon coffee and cake.

You'll want to take dinner pretty late, which means there'll be time to visit the opera, where upstairs standing room costs only a couple of dollars and allows a clear—if distant—view of the stage and access to the best acoustics in the house. At that price and with tired legs you won't feel compelled to stay for the entire show. Around 10pm you may descend into the bowels of the city and point to your favourite sausages or slices of spiced beef in the Esterhazykeller, which is a maze of caverns crammed with noisy benches. Austrian wine tends to taste like sour apple juice, so you'll probably drink beer.

After a few days of this I had the strong suspicion that my bloodstream was becoming as clogged as my digestive system, and I decided to take a stand. The Majestat restaurant at the Hotel Imperial (where Hitler stayed after the unification of Austria and Germany in 1938) has a high reputation in the gourmet books, so I went there for dinner and said to the waiter: 'Do you think the chef could do us a plate of mixed vegetables?'

Waiter: 'Anything you want.'

Me: 'What is in season now?'

W: 'We have herrings done five different ways.'

Me: 'Well yes, but do you have any vegetables?'

W: 'Anything you want.'

He backed rapidly away, and returned a minute later

with the head waiter, who said: 'I'm sorry, what did you want?'

Me: 'A plate of mixed vegetables.'

HW: 'You do not like meat?'

Me: 'Not today. I was hoping the chef could do something interesting with vegetables.'

HW: 'You want English style?'

Me: 'What does that mean?'

HW: 'Boiled vegetables.'

Me: 'No, no, not boiled vegetables. We wondered if the chef could do a few different vegetables in different ways.'

HW: 'Anything you want.'

The two waiters disappeared, and returned 15 minutes later with herrings done five different ways and a platter containing spinach puree with a poached quail egg, tiny zucchini, steamed carrots, sautéed potatoes, fried spring onions, green asparagus mousse and white asparagus wrapped in ham. They watched as we two foreign eccentrics tucked in gleefully. We felt good enough after that to order cream cakes for dessert. And the next night we were ready to face a restaurant called the Gulasch Museum, at which you are given a fat book of colour photos and asked to choose the stew that most attracts you. We knew better than to ask for vegetables there.

There is, as it turns out, an excellent vegetarian restaurant in Vienna, called Siddhartha, and there is also a restaurant which manages to incorporate Germanic generosity, French finesse and a reasonable fibre and vitamin content. It's called Steirereck. Bonus dishes keep being presented during your meal: an asparagus soup in a tiny cup, a sort of chicken nugget on a saucer, a strip of salmon wrapped round cream cheese and, miracle of miracles, a 'vegetable cocktail'—tiny pieces of capsicum, zucchini and garlic in a spicy stock. You barely have the appetite for the roast rabbit on noodles (with its tiny liver and kidney on the side) and the foie gras with a red cabbage jelly, or the poppy and apricot ravioli and the cream cheese dumplings and the pears and prunes poached in cinnamon. But somehow you struggle through, because, after all, this is not gluttony. You're doing this to absorb, and therefore understand, a whole culture.

6 · FREUD'S FLAT, VIENNA

Sigmund Freud's walking stick, his tweed cap and his travelling rug are hanging in the front hall of his apartment at number 19 Berggasse, Vienna. This would suggest that the Doktor-Professor is at home, which is just as well, because if ever there was a suitable case for treatment, it's the capital of Austria.

Vienna is a city preoccupied with death, with one of the highest suicide rates in Europe; a centre of wealth, espionage, repression, smuggling, double dealing, double standards, sentimental music, over-blown architecture and overwhelming cream cakes. And perhaps for the same reasons, it's also a city which has encouraged revolutionary ideas, leaps of the imagination and wondrous eccentricity.

Only this city could have provided the hothouse in which the theories of the most significant figure of the 20th century could flourish. And only this city could have moulded the second most significant figure: Adolf Hitler.

Hitler was born Adolf Shicklgrüber in northern Austria, and spent his teenage years, between 1904 and 1913, living in various men's doss houses in Vienna. He failed the entry requirements for an art course at the Vienna Academy, and made a bare living as a carpet beater. Hitler wrote later, in *Mein Kampf:* 'Vienna was and remained for me the hardest but also the most thorough school in my life'. He said his basic views were formed in Vienna 'at so early a time under the pressure of fate and through my own learning'.

Sigmund Freud practised medicine in Vienna from 1886 till 1938. It's not outlandish to imagine that Hitler and Freud passed each other in the street many times in this concentrated city, or nodded to each other in the Cafe Landtmann (where at a third table Lenin might have been earning his living as a professional chess player). Perhaps Shicklgrüber, dressed in the long black overcoat given to him by a Jewish tailor, may have even trudged up the stairs to the first floor of 19 Berggasse to do a spot of carpet cleaning for Martha Freud. If only the Doktor had turned around and said, 'You look like a troubled young man—come and have a chat with me', 20th century history would have been very different.

Freud himself professed to hate Vienna for its narrow-mindedness and anti-semitism, but for 47 years he stayed in 19 Berggasse and interviewed patients in the surgery attached to his flat. He saw Vienna through its most interesting times: the collapse of the Hapsburg Empire that once ruled all of eastern Europe, the civil war between the socialists and the conservatives in the early 1930s, and the ultimate triumph of Hitler's ideas. His family had a hard time persuading him to leave for his own safety in 1938. The Nazi administration put him through immense bureaucracy before finally giving him permission to take the train, and then, at the last moment, another petty official arrived with another petty form for him to sign. It was a declaration to be shown to the rest of the world that the Nazis had never ill-treated him. Freud looked at it, signed, and added a postscript: 'I can most heartily recommend the Gestapo to everyone'. The official had no sense of irony, and went away delighted, as Freud headed for London and the last of his 82 years. His four sisters, who had to stay behind, died in concentration camps in 1941.

Most visitors to Vienna these days have Mozart on their minds, and they head immediately for the apartment in Domgasse where he wrote *The Marriage of Figaro*, or his alleged grave in St Mark Cemetery. Then they go in search of Beethoven (no less than nine houses in central Vienna are claimed as his former residence) or Schubert or Haydn.

Visitors who prefer kings to composers wander through the rococo remains of the Austro-Hungarian Empire—vast draughty palaces filled with displays of weapons and uniforms. They may divert themselves with some study of the burial practices of the Hapsburg Emperors and Empresses. The royal bodies are in vaults under the Capuchin Church, but the royal hearts have all been removed and are kept in the Augustin Church adjoining the Imperial Palace. And the royal entrails are kept in a third shrine—the catacombs under St Stephen's Cathedral. The Viennese see nothing odd in this dissection, but then, Vienna is the only city in Europe with a museum devoted to undertaking.

My pilgrimage was in search of the origins of psychoanalysis. I wanted to climb the stairs that had once been trod by the Wolf Man, the Rat Man, Little Hans and Dora—Freud's most famous case studies—and by Carl

Jung, who first travelled to Vienna from Zurich in March 1907. On the day of his arrival at 19 Berggasse, Jung spent 13 hours in non-stop conversation with Freud, describing him later as 'extremely intelligent, shrewd and altogether remarkable'.

Since then, Freud's reputation has taken a bashing. His data collection was unscientific, his treatment methods don't work, and much of his theory is mumbo-jumbo based on his own hangups. Nevertheless, he is responsible for spreading the most powerful idea of our time: the unconscious mind. He persuaded us that our behaviour is driven by forces we do not understand, and those forces are within ourselves.

Everybody at the end of the 20th century speaks Freud. Our dreams are full of hidden meanings. We brand each other paranoid, ego-driven, oedipal, latent, repressed, fixated and inhibited. Artists sublimate lust and politicians sublimate aggression. Men have castration anxiety and women have penis envy. But then again, as Freud pointed out when told that his addiction was actually a phallic symbol, 'sometimes a cigar is just a cigar'. (The symbol got its revenge in the end. Freud died in 1939 after 15 years of agony from cancer of the jaw. It was the only way his unconscious mind could stop him blabbing any more secrets.)

In a book called *The Freud Reader*, Peter Gay writes: 'Sigmund Freud—along with Karl Marx, Charles Darwin and Albert Einstein—is among that small handful of supreme makers of the 20th century whose works should be our prized possessions'. Gay says Freud enraged people by convincing them that humans are a long way from gods. 'Copernicus had shown that the earth, and hence man, is not at the centre of the universe; Darwin had linked mankind to the animal kingdom; and now

Freud had demonstrated that reason is not master in his own house.' (Hitler for one, found this implication of Freud's theories objectionable. In May 1933, just weeks after Hitler was installed as Germany's Chancellor, the Nazis held a book burning rally in Berlin, at which Freud's texts were thrown into the fire by students chanting: 'Against soul-disintegrating exaggeration of the instinctual life, for the nobility of the human soul! I commit to the flames the writings of Sigmund Freud'.)

So I've rung the bell, I've climbed the stairs, and I've been admitted to Freud's front hall by one of the psychology students who take turns looking after the flat these days. I am standing where a party of Nazi stormtroopers were greeted by Martha Freud when they raided the flat on 15 March 1938—two days after Hitler had announced the 'unification' of Germany and Austria. 'She treated them as ordinary visitors, inviting them to put their rifles in the sections of the hall stand reserved for umbrellas,' wrote Freud's son Martin later. 'And although the invitation was not accepted, her courtesy and courage had had a good effect. Father, too, had retained his invincible poise, leaving his sofa where he had been resting to join mother in the living room, where he sat calmly in his armchair throughout the raid.' The stormtroopers confiscated all passports and 6000 schillings in cash (the equivalent of several hundred dollars in these days). Freud remarked: 'I have never taken so much for a single visit'.

I am shown into a parlour, where, in a roped-off area, I see a red velvet couch. 'Is that *the* couch?' I ask. 'Yes, that's Freud's couch,' says the student. 'The couch where his patients lay?' I ask. 'Ah no, this is the couch where the patients sat while they waited to see him. *That* couch is in his house in London.' And indeed, it turns out that the flat at 19 Berggasse is nearly empty, because most of Freud's furniture followed him to his new home at 20 Maresfield Gardens, Hampstead, in 1938. (Naturally I made that pilgrimage too. The couch turns out to be covered with a red and black oriental rug which must have made life difficult for patients with dust allergies. The keepers of the London house will also show you home movies made of Freud in his last years, which reveal him as a jolly invalid laughing with his dog and his grand-children, and they'll play you a broadcast he made for the BBC late in 1938, in which he summarises his life: 'I discovered some new and important facts about the Unconscious in psychic life, the role of instinctual urges and so on ... I had to pay heavily for this bit of good luck. People did not believe in my facts and thought my theories unsavoury. Resistance was strong and unrelent-ing. In the end I succeeded in acquiring pupils and build-ing up an International Psycho-Analytic Association. But the struggle is not yet over'.)

The starkness of 19 Berggasse somehow makes being there a more powerful experience. You see the chair in which Freud sat to write up his case studies and puff on his cigars. You see some of the small Greek and Egyptian sculptures he liked to fondle as he listened to his patients' outpourings. And on the wall you see his mother's pass-port from 1859, with the great seal of Emperor Franz Josef, King of Hungary, Bohemia, Lombardy, Venice, Galicia, Lodomerien and Illyrien. How many of those names will be individual nations again by the turn of this century?

When you leave Freud's flat, you can't help noticing psychiatric symptoms everywhere in Vienna. Embedded in the paving stones on the main shopping street, Kart-nerstrasse, is a marble sign that reads: 'They said it was the land of milk and honey. Now they say it's the land of money. Who ever thought they could make that stick—Bob Dylan'. You regularly bump into elaborate memorials to the victims of the Nazis—yet Nazism was not something imposed on the Austrians from outside. Ecstatic crowds greeted Hitler's arrival in February 1938, having first rounded up Jews and forced them to scrub the streets. In a referendum held on 10 April 1938, the voters of Austria were 99 percent in favour of adopting Hitler's laws (not that they had any choice). And in the 1980s, in the full knowledge that he had been a Nazi agent, the citizens of Austria voted overwhelmingly for Kurt Waldheim as their President.

Even Vienna's obsession with Freud could be seen as a symptom which he would have found worthy of analysis. There's a park named after him, adjoining the university, with a stone inscribed: 'The voice of reason is soft'. There's a bust of him in the university courtyard, inscribed with a quote from *Oedipus Rex*: 'He who solved the notorious riddle and became a mighty, powerful man'. There's a housing complex for low-income earners named after him (somewhat overshadowed by the housing complex named after Karl Marx, which still proudly bears the scars inflicted by the right-wing government's mortar shells during the 1934 civil war).

And in a carpark in the outer suburb of Bellevue, on the site of a guesthouse where Freud used to holiday, there's a plaque that says: 'In this house on July 24th, 1895, the Secret of Dreams was revealed to Dr Sigmund Freud'. This is a nice piece of irony by the city planners, because the wording deliberately echoes a letter written in 1900 by Freud, when he was doubtful if his research would ever amount to anything. He asked a friend: 'Do you really believe that some day, on this house, one will read on a marble tablet: "Here revealed itself, on July 24, 1895, the secret of dreams to Dr. Sigm. Freud"? At this moment I see little prospect of it'.

Continuing my search for Vienna's psyche, I spent a day wandering around the city with an artist and designer named Friedensreich Hundertwasser. Of partly Jewish background, he was forced to join the Hitler Youth as a child to protect his family from investigation by the Nazis. When he began painting after the war, he changed his name from Friedrich Stowasser to a name which literally means 'Kingdom-of-peace Hundred-waters'. By the 1970s he had made a fortune from posters, cards and books of his riotously coloured landscapes and cityscapes. Vienna has established a museum devoted to his work, in a building he designed himself. He took me up to its roof, which is covered with earth and grass, so that I could meet his two pet rabbits. You could say Hundertwasser is eccentric, hyperactive and arrogant, or that he is a visionary. Now in his 70s, he inspires in the Viennese something like the reaction Freud must have provoked in his time: a mixture of admiration, amazement and anger.

I asked Hundertwasser if he had a theory on why Vienna has such a high suicide rate (25 per 100,000—double that of America or Australia). It turns out he has a theory on everything. He said it's because of the prevailing conformism of the populace and the determination of the state to regiment every aspect of life: 'When you take away the impetus of creativity of every citizen, then people tend to think they are not needed, there's no demand for their ideas, and they become apathetic. Most suicides come out of apathy. In Vienna, people don't have to fight, everything is done for them, ready-made. From birth to death, everything is pre-established, nothing can happen to you, you don't have to think'.

Hundertwasser is being a bit unfair in condemning Austria's administration for the social safety net it provides. Not everything about Vienna is cushioned and timid. The city has been surprisingly receptive, for example, to Hundertwasser's crusades against conformist architecture. He began in the early 70s with a campaign for what he calls 'window rights', which he describes thus: 'The occupant of an apartment must have the right to lean out of his window and to decorate the outer wall as it suits him as far as his arm can reach, so that one can see at a distance that an individual human being is living there'.

Next he decided he wanted to create whole buildings. 'The city is uniform, flat, dictatorial, so I thought something must be done,' he says. 'I am not an architect, not a politician, I have no power, only to make my ideas known in demonstrations and speeches and writing and models.' His campaign worked again. In 1977 the Mayor of Vienna asked him to collaborate with the city's architects in designing an apartment block for low-income people on a vacant site near the city centre. The result is the extraordinary Hundertwasser Haus, on the corner of Lowengasse and Kegelgasse. From a distance you'd think it was a melting set of multicoloured plasticine. Colours are splashed over it in waves of paint and fragments of tiles. The roof is covered with a layer of earth and grass, because, says Hundertwasser, that's the best insulation and it brings the occupants closer to nature. The floors in the 52 apartments undulate in gentle bumps because, he says, 'an uneven floor is a melody to the feet' (and Hundertwasser has designed uneven furniture to match). Large trees grow from *inside* the rooms and stretch their limbs through the windows to the sun. Hundertwasser calls them 'tree tenants—ambassadors of the free forest to the city'.

The block has become a pilgrimage site for architecture students, which amuses Hundertwasser. 'Architects are trained to copy horrible boxes, and to work with rulers and t-squares,' he says. 'Every architect could do what I do, but they are afraid. They say no to all dreams of romance and beauty. A trained architect is a qualified killer. He killed his own dreams, so then he is allowed to create buildings for mankind.'

The Vienna city council was so pleased with the Hundertwasser Haus that they next asked him to tackle the city's biggest eyesore—an industrial waste incinerator. Hundertwasser says he accepted the assignment without a fee because 'visual pollution is more poisonous than any other pollution, because it kills the soul, the self-confidence. People around ugly sites are more disposed to suicide, to alcoholism, to drug addiction, vandalism, all kinds of sicknesses. My buildings may be more expensive to build but they last longer and they save money in the end, because otherwise the community has to pay for all the negative effects of the ugliness.'

The new incinerator emerged in 1989 as a surrealist fantasy, with a giant golden bulb around the chimney, a curving blue roof like a tent, mock picture windows in yellow and red, and a chequerboard pattern around its body. It has become another tourist attraction and architectural sacred site.

Most of Hundertwasser's current projects are done for free. 'Fortunately my paintings are of some value and the income from my books and my graphics lets me survive. My reward now is to make people joyful and give them back some living quality and some fulfilment of their longing for romance and beauty. I prove that things can be done.'

Hundertwasser says he is fond of Vienna but every

few months its relentless 'cosiness' becomes too much for him. He feels he is suffocating. Then he goes off to empty his mind at a large wilderness property he has bought in the Bay of Islands area of New Zealand—'about as far from Vienna as it is possible to be'.

When I think about Vienna, I have three pictures in my mind: Hundertwasser up on the grassy roof of his museum calling to his rabbits; those home movies of Freud laughing with his grandchildren in the courtyard of 19 Berggasse; and newsreel footage of thousands of people cheering Adolf Hitler as he stands on the balcony of the Neue Berg palace. In their placid way, the Viennese rejoice in an atmosphere that has given the world both the peaks and the pits of the human spirit.

7 · GRASSE, FRANCE

In one sense, the southern French town of Grasse could be described as the most familiar place on earth. The one sense is that of smell. Surrounded by fields full of roses, carnations, jasmine, mimosa, orange blossom and lavender, Grasse is the source of most of the world's great perfumes. It follows then that the most influential person on earth might be the man known in Grasse as Le Nez (pronounced le nay). It means 'the nose'.

The Nose is a mysterious figure. He (and it is always a he) is comparable, I'm inclined to think, with the comic book hero The Shadow, whose slogan was 'Who knows what secrets lurk within the hearts of men? The Shadow knows'. The Nose knows as well. The secrets were probably passed on to him by his father, and honed over three years of sniffing at France's National School of Perfumers in Versailles, near Paris. Just think for a moment how many smells you can distinguish and name. One hundred, maybe? The Nose has learnt to distinguish 315 fragrances by the time he completes his training and returns to Grasse to start making million dollar decisions for his perfume company.

The most you're likely to see of The Nose is his white-coated back through the glass wall that is between you, in the observation room, and him, in the sterile laboratory of a company such as Fragonard, where he sits before an array of tiny bottles, called the Organ because it looks like an old-fashioned church organ with all stops out. This is where the Nose creates his harmonies. There are fewer than 100 people alive on earth who have skills approaching those of the man whose back you are observing, and only 15 currently practising in France.

For all his highly paid talent, The Nose lives like a monk. He must never smoke, never drink alcohol or coffee, and never eat garlicky or spicy foods, because any of those vices would interfere with his ability to detect and concoct exquisite fragrances. He works only three hours a day, because sniffing at such intensity is exhausting, and his skills decline rapidly with fatigue. The world's most expensive perfume, 'Joy', was the result of four years' work by a Nose somewhere in Grasse (but his identity is secret). A Nose is usually burnt out by 40.

Traditionally, Grasse was France's leather tanning centre; it started distilling perfumes in 1595 to hide the stench of the hides in ladies' gloves. But wild and crazy women started wanting to put the fragrances on themselves as well as on their gloves, and a new industry was born. Now the making of smells creates employment for 70 percent of the 15,000 citizens of Grasse.

In the 20th century, the sexiest scents in the world have originated from Grasse's 30 perfume factories, even if the credit for them has been claimed elsewhere. When an American company decides to market a perfume associated with a star such as Elizabeth Taylor, they will retain an organisation such as Fragonard to develop it. Down in Grasse, the Nose sets to work anonymously at his organ of essences, blending microscopic quantities of as many as 200 odours until the result meets the psychological and aesthetic requirements. Fragonard hands over the secret formula to the purchasing company, which develops the packaging and the publicity and charges a fortune for the result.

Fragonard, meanwhile, quietly produces its own version of the fragrance its Nose invented, and will sell it in small quantities to those who make the pilgrimage to Grasse. Thus if you could not afford the perfume 'Paris'—supposedly the creation of Yves St Laurent but actually the creation of Fragonard's Nose—you could buy something almost identical to it from the Fragonard factory under the name 'Emilie'. Their version of 'Oscar de la Renta' is called 'Banjo'. Their version of 'L'Air du Temps' is 'Moment Vole'. And their version of 'Anais Anais' is called just 'Fragonard'.

You can tour the factories of Fragonard, Galimard and Molinard (there's not much else to do in town), and see them 'capturing the souls' of flowers by dropping thousands of petals into a warm soup of pork and beef fats, which is later treated with alcohol and distilled to produce a concentrated essence. The process is called maceration. The petals come from the vast flower fields surrounding Grasse, and from all over France, varying with the season. In April, for example, they macerate orange blossoms, in May, roses, in July, jasmine, in August, tuberoses. One tonne of orange blossoms produces one litre of essence. One bottle of jasmine perfume requires 60 million petals. It takes 900,000 rosebuds to make a kilo of rose essence. Into which the Nose might then need to stir some genital secretions from cats, a dab of musk from Tibetan goats, and a smidgin of whale vomit. No, I lie, the perfumiers at Grasse assured me that in recent years they've stopped using ambergris from whales.

The Fragonard Nose remains anonymous behind his glass wall, but occasionally other great Noses give an insight into their work. Jacques Cavallier is The Nose for Lancome, and is best known for creating a fragrance called 'Poeme'. 'My father was a Nose and when I was a child he trained me,' he says. 'It is memory training and it's really very simple if you have a lot of time. You start by smelling different raw materials, only natural raw materials. After two years, you start to learn the blend of different materials in order to reproduce what nature is giving to us. After three or four years you must study all the great perfumes—such as Chanel No. 5 (the first designer perfume, created on the instructions of Coco Chanel in 1923). You have to learn how these perfumes are built and understand the ideas behind them. All smells can be good for a perfume. Materials sometimes used to create perfumes don't smell so good. Imdol is in almost every flower, and it smells like shit. But this smell, this product, gives all the bloom of flowers.'

The novel *Perfume*, by Patrick Suskind, tells the story of the finest Nose the world has ever known (able to distinguish more than 1000 smells). This bogey man, who has no odour of his own, becomes obsessed with distilling the essence of a young woman, even if it means killing her. Suskind says of Grasse in the late 18th century: 'This equally homely and self-confident place was ... the uncontested centre for production of and commerce in scents, perfumes, soaps and oils. The town was the Rome of scents, the promised land of perfumers, and the man who had not earned his spurs here did not rightfully bear the title of perfumer ... The town was divided lengthwise by a brook where tanners washed their hides and afterwards spread them out to dry. The odour was so pungent that many a guest lost his appetite for his meal. Nevertheless, however filthy, cramped and slovenly, the town was bursting with the bustle of commerce'.

Nowadays little has changed, except that the brook has been bricked over and the odour of hides has been replaced by the odour of car exhausts (the centre of Grasse is a permanent traffic jam of cars driving from Cannes and Nice into Provence, and vice versa).

On the evening after my tour of Parfumerie Fragonard, as I was sitting in Grasse's comfortable Amphitryon restaurant eating cutlets of lamb that had fed on lavender, I found myself thinking of how a local paper might headline a story about Fragonard's perfumer having his secrets discovered, leaving town, and being replaced: 'Nose blown, runs; new Nose picked'.

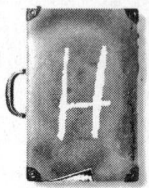

8 · HOLLYWOODLAND

About three kilometres from the spot where Julia Roberts picked up Richard Gere (or was it the other way round?) in *Pretty Woman*, I'm doing a bit of bush-walking in the Hollywood Hills. I'm on a sandy ochre track with a green lake below me and a scrubby mountainside above me. The air is filled with birdsong. I've already seen two rabbits amongst the purple sage, but not yet the coyotes or mountain lions that occasionally wander through the area (according to the sworn testimony of a friend who lives just down the hill). In half an hour of walking, the only human life I've seen is one red and sweaty jogger.

It's the sort of landscape where I expect to encounter Wyatt Earp and his posse, but what I actually see as I round the next boulder is a six-storey mansion built into the hillside, painted dark red with wide yellow stripes. As I walk closer, I see that the words 'Castello del Lago' are painted on the wall near its gate. Here amongst this glorious isolation I have found the California home of Madonna, with external colouring designed by her brother. Back in the 1930s it was Bugsy Siegel's gambling casino.

And in case I have trouble remembering where I am, I can see behind the mansion, higher up the hill, the HOLLYWOOD sign, built to advertise a real estate company in 1923, with letters 18 metres high and 10 metres wide. The sign said HOLLYWOODLAND (which was the name of the company) until the last syllable fell down, and the shortened version was restored in the late 1970s at a cost of $250,000 per letter from the pockets of local donors such as Hugh Hefner and Andy Williams.

The only person I know who admits to liking Los Angeles is me, and part of the reason is surreal experiences such as bushwalking with birdsong just three kilometres from one of the most polluted urban sprawls on the planet. Most outsiders seem to share the view of Westbrook Pegler, who described it as 'that big, sprawling, incoherent, shapeless, slobbering, civic idiot in the family of American communities', or Dorothy Parker, who called it '72 suburbs in search of a city'. More recently, Val Kilmer (an occasional Batman) gave this analysis: 'Violence comes out of the blue here. I've had friends who were carjacked, all kinds of things. Successful felons, criminals, love LA. It's so big, there's so many freeways to get on after you do your score. Because of its possibilities, LA's the most sorrowful city in the world'.

But Kilmer is talking about a real place. I'm talking about a fantasy world—a state of mind called Hollywoodland rather than a postcode called Hollywood. My preferred description of LA comes from Frank Lloyd Wright: 'a circus without a tent'. The circus is movies and television. Its acts generate the folklore with which every-one in the western world now grows up. The mythical creatures that populate our unconscious minds are no longer imprinted by the brothers Grimm and Hans Christian Anderson and Lewis Carroll. They are created by Hollywoodland. That's why it's an essential place.

It just happens that the universe we glimpse in films and television intersects with the real world more often in greater Los Angeles than in any other city. I could, I suppose, list the Crown Hotel in Amersham, just outside London, as an essential place, because it's where Charles and Carrie (Hugh Grant and Andie McDowell) had their first one night stand in *Four Weddings and a Funeral*. Or the sewers of Vienna, because *The Third Man* had its climax there. But I'd be hard pressed to find other manifestations of Hollywoodland in those locations. You can't beat LA for sheer concentration of movie imagery. And I don't mean the kind of spots you'd see on the Graveline Bus Tour of places where actors died. I'm as curious as the next fan about the tombs and homes and restaurants of the stars, but I'm more interested in sites sacred to purely fictional characters. My LA is where ET landed, where the Terminator sought its prey, where Marty McFly drove a sports car back to the future, where Macarthur Park is melting in the dark, where the Beverly Hillbillies settled, where Vincent Vega took the boss's wife for a five dollar milkshake, and where the crew of the Starship Enterprise beamed down repeatedly (because LA is very good at looking like an alien planet).

To get the best out of LA, I would argue, it's neces-sary to choose the bits most congenial to your particular interests and shuttle rapidly between them, ignoring all the rest. In my case, those bits are Santa Monica, West Hollywood, Melrose Avenue, and what the locals call 'the

Downtown'. I eat and swim and sometimes stay at Santa Monica, I wander and buy junk on Melrose, I bushwalk and sometimes stay in the Hollywood Hills, and I seek myths at the Downtown. The bits I ignore include Disneyland (if I want to entertain kids, Universal Studios has shorter queues); Orange County (unless I'm going to the Richard Nixon Museum, an oasis of strangeness in a desert of suburbia); the San Fernando Valley (unless I'm making a pilgrimage to the house where ET hid—7121 Lonzo Street, Tujunga); and Pasadena (unless I want to eat in Kevin Costner's restaurant, Twin Palms).

A complaint about Los Angeles attributed to Dorothy Parker was that 'there's no *there*, there', which is a typical Manhattanite's reaction to the fact that there doesn't seem to be anything you could call an inner city. In fact, *there* is the Downtown, but travellers rarely visit it because they think they'll be subjected to degrading sights and violent confrontations. Certainly the streets are full of beggars, and I'm not sure I'd be comfortable wandering around at night, but there's much to see during the day.

I went in search of the Bradbury Building, corner of Third Street and Broadway, which was the home of the puppetmaker in *Blade Runner*, and the scene of the final confrontation between Deckard (Harrison Ford) and the replicant (Rutger Hauer). In the film, it's a partly derelict structure, with layers of internal balconies under a massive skylight. To my surprise, I found it had been recently restored to its 1893 glory, with yellow brickwork and iron filigree, and lamps glowing through sconces of translucent stone. It now houses various law firms and the offices of the California State Treasurer.

The two blocks around the Bradbury are undergoing big renovation, with the grandest of the gothic 1920s skyscrapers and cinemas getting scrubdowns and new noses on their gargoyles. There's also a modern surge, with high-security glass towers starting to surround the deco dinosaurs. And in the middle, the most unexpected discovery in this city of surprises: a fresh food market with stalls overflowing with fruit, vegetables, fish and home-made sausages. It would be a normal sight in a French or Italian village square, but in LA people are supposed to buy their food wrapped in plastic from supermarkets. As it turns out, the Grand Central Produce Market has been functioning on this spot since 1917, back when LA was still trying to be a real city. Its main customers these days are the local Mexican community, which accounts for the colour and diversity of the produce (though not for the thriving 'Chow Mein Chop Suey' stall in the middle). If you want to find out what the Mexicans do with the produce, wander down nearby Olvera Street around lunchtime.

Just down from the produce market, on the corner of Hill Street and 4th Street, is a monument to municipal madness—one of the sparkling stations of the new LA subway. It was built in the 1980s out of guilt, by a city tired of being accused of destroying its public transport system to make way for the car. Descend the escalator and you'll walk through lino-floored caverns that are eerily clean. That's because the subway is empty of human life. Are the fares too high? Hardly—the machines lining the walls advertise tickets at 25 cents a journey. The problem is that the subway doesn't go anywhere that people want to travel. The business types who work in the Downtown's office blocks live many miles away and drive into guarded carparks under their towers. The locals use buses. The few people walking round down there are probably doing mental reconstructions of the final scenes in *Speed*.

A stroll around the perimeter of the Downtown

offers much to reward the fantasy scholar, in particular the 1928 City Hall, which was police headquarters in *Dragnet* and the office of *The Daily Planet*—the tall building to be leapt in a single bound—in the original *Superman* TV series. There's also the 1923 Biltmore Hotel on Grand Street, where they filmed bits of *Ghostbusters*, *The Fabulous Baker Boys* and *Vertigo*, and the Spanish-deco Union Station, where the legendary trans-America trains of the 1920s began and ended their journeys. Raymond Babbitt (Dustin Hoffman) set off from there at the end of *Rain Man*.

After a day on foot in the Downtown you can, with clear conscience, climb back in your car and explore more scattered pleasures. On the way to Hollywood you'll drive through Macarthur Park, which looks like an inverted wedding cake and is sparkling in the sun, and the LaBrea Tar Pits, a puddle of prehistoric ooze studded with fibreglass mammoths, into which Jack Slater (Arnold Schwarzenegger) tumbled in *The Last Action Hero*. At Century City you can examine Fox Plaza, the skyscraper hijacked by terrorists and rescued by John McClane (Bruce Willis) in *Die Hard*, and the Century Plaza Towers, which were the headquarters of the Blue Moon Detective Agency in *Moonlighting* (with Willis and Cybill Shepherd).

The *Blade Runner* trail will lead you into the Hollywood Hills, to a boxy fortress designed by Frank Lloyd Wright (see Chapter 3)—the Ennis-Brown House at 2607 Glendower Avenue. Inside, you'll recognise the Aztec tiles as the motif round Deckard's apartment and the elevator as the one Deckard was walking towards as he reflected on the words 'Too bad she won't live. But then again, who does?'

If you continue north, to 500 South Buena Vista

Street in the area the TV series *Laugh In* used to call 'beautiful downtown Burbank', you'll reach the biggest myth factory of them all—the Disney studios. This complex was built in 1940 with profits from the world's first full-length animated film, *Snow White and the Seven Dwarfs*. The main administration building has a top modelled on a Greek temple, but instead of columns, the roof is supported by massive sculptures of Happy, Sleepy, Sneezy, Grumpy, Bashful, Dopey and Doc.

The place is known as Moushwitz or Duckau because of the way its executives treat the workers. In the early 1990s, it was the site of what those executives thought was the major breakthrough in modern motion pictures. One of Disney's script assessors, Christopher Vogler, wrote a memo to his bosses outlining what he perceived to be the essential ingredients in any successful movie. Drawing on the theories of the psychoanalyst Carl Jung and the mythologist Joseph Campbell, he spun a plausible yarn about the human need for heroes and journeys and challenges. The executives went ape—finally they had the formula they'd been seeking all their careers, not to mention a whole new jargon for labelling their products. They passed the memo to their writers, directors and producers, and when a story idea arrived without a Call To Adventure or a Mentor or a Supreme Ordeal, they wanted to know why.

When the media found out about Vogler's 'Practical Guide', they attacked it as the source of the standardisation that seemed to be fossilising modern movies. Vogler says he was blamed for 'every flop from *Ishtar* to *Howard the Duck*, as well as for the hit *Back To The Future*'. The media theorised that 'lazy, illiterate studio executives, eager to find a quick bucks formula, had seized upon the Practical Guide as a cure-all and were stifling creativity with a technology the executives hadn't bothered to understand'.

But the criticism obviously rolled off Vogler's back, because he expanded the original seven-page memo to a book of 315 pages, called *The Writer's Journey*. He argues that deep in our unconscious minds there's a need for stories and characters that follow a particular pattern. The pattern goes through 12 stages. We find the hero in The Ordinary World (stage 1). Then he or she receives a Call To Adventure (2), to seek something or someone, but he/she refuses (3). Then a wise old Mentor offers help (4) and the hero crosses The First Threshold (5). On the journey, the hero encounters Tests, Allies and Enemies (6) and is allowed to have a bit of fun with Tricksters, Shapeshifters and Wise Fools. But soon he or she must make the Approach to the Inmost Cave (7) via assorted Threshold Guardians, and face The Supreme Ordeal (8). The hero obtains The Reward (9), starts on The Road Back (10), has another ordeal which leads to a form of Resurrection (11) and finally makes a triumphant Return With The Elixir (12).

You can see how this applies to films such as *The Wizard of Oz*, *Star Wars* and *Raiders of the Lost Ark*, and out there in Burbank, the Disney company used Vogler's formula quite self-consciously to generate *Aladdin*, *Beauty and the Beast* and *The Lion King*. But Vogler says it's equally useful in explaining the success of less traditional fantasies such as *Pulp Fiction*, or *Pretty Woman*, or even *Four Weddings and a Funeral*. They all have to be seen as mythical journeys, just like our trip through Hollywoodland.

On your way back from Burbank (the Inmost Cave?) you'll want to take Mulholland Drive past the homes of Jack Nicholson, Warren Beatty, Sharon Stone and Marlon Brando and examine the house on stilts (number 7436) that Martin Riggs (Mel Gibson) pulled down in *Lethal Weapon 2*. As Mulholland turns into a dirt track you'll pass a sign saying 'This canyon has been adopted by Bette Midler', which apparently means she pays local school-kids to keep the footpaths tidy.

Canyons aren't the only things the stars are adopting. They're also becoming the proud parents of restaurants. Status in The Big Orange these days is no longer based on who you know—it's based on knowing who owns where you're eating. People pack restaurants because they belong to actors.

Kevin Costner's sprawling bungalow-style restaurant called Twin Palms in Pasadena claims to offer 'southern French food', which seems to include cottage pie, Caesar salad and seafood cocktail. Denzel Washington and Eddie Murphy own the elegant Georgia, on Melrose Avenue, which has a black and beautiful clientele. The cooking is deep southern, specialising in pork, okra, black eye peas, salt, sugar and chicken fat. Whoopi Goldberg and Joe Pesci own Eclipse, also on Melrose, which offers trendy Italian food and whole fish baked in wood-fired ovens. LA Farm, on Olympic Avenue, Santa Monica, is attached to George Lucas's Skywalker Studios, so you might find yourself sharing a pasta with Jabba The Hut.

Bikini in Santa Monica was the place where Chili Palmer (John Travolta) threw a thug down the stairs in *Get Shorty*. The chef uses food to paint works of art on the plate, making you fearful of spoiling the symmetry of the tiny carved vegetables and the swirls and arrows of pureed avocado and chilli powder. It was reported that Dustin Hoffman looked at his meal and said: 'I already have a Lichtenstein on my wall. I don't need one on my plate'.

And at Modada on Melrose Avenue you can experience something like the meal served in *Like Water For*

Chocolate—a dish called Erotic Chicken, 'roasted whole boneless baby chicken stuffed with forest mushrooms on a flower of purple endive with a rose petal sauce'. In a spirit of irony, Modada features 'retro' dishes that fell out of fashion soon after our parents got married, for example the romantic 'Curry Cheese Fondue For Two with accessories of dried salami, roasted mini potatoes, slices of granny smith apples, and day old French bread'. It's amusing at first sight, but eating with your tongue in your cheek soon becomes messy.

Your choice of accommodation in LA can also keep you inside Hollywoodland. If you're old and rich, you'd stay at the Beverly Wilshire at the bottom of Rodeo Drive, where Edward (Richard Gere) took Vivian (Julia Roberts) for her week's employment in *Pretty Woman* and Axel Foley (Eddie Murphy) conned everybody in *Beverly Hills Cop*; or at the pink Beverly Hills Hotel, where Marilyn Monroe slept—separately—with John Kennedy and Robert Kennedy. Even if you're not staying there, it's worth a stroll through the corridors and a prowl round the pool to see who is doing deals in the cabanas. Howard Hughes had a nervous breakdown in bungalow number 4.

The more economically-minded traveller might prefer a pleasantly seedy spot called the Chateau Marmont at 8221 Sunset Boulevard. Since it opened in 1929, the Marmont has been a temporary home for entertainers on the way up or on the way down, such as Greta Garbo, Warren Beatty, Jim Morrison, Roman Polanski, Bob Dylan and Dustin Hoffman. It became hot accommodation in 1982 when John Belushi died of a drug overdose in its bungalow number 3. Bungalow 3 was busy when I booked, but room 21 in the main building certainly smelt as if someone had died in it—not recently, and not violently, but quietly, over a long time, perhaps while awaiting a comeback in the movie business. The bathroom tap wouldn't stop dripping, the headboard of my bed rattled whenever I moved, and there was a hole in the plastic round the airconditioning box, which let in a stream of dust particles. But two complimentary 'sensitive latex' condoms, packaged to look like gold coins, were provided in the bathroom, along with the little bottle of Institute Swiss Ginseng Shampoo. And I was allowed to swim in the oval pool next to the bungalows, where the preferred style is backstroke so you can watch the vapour trails in the polluted pink evening sky.

The Marmont is the ideal place from which to undertake a walking tour of Sunset Boulevard, which is the spine of Hollywoodland. Directly across the road is a twice-lifesize statue of Bullwinkle Moose holding up Rocket J. Squirrel. The statue marks the animation studios of Jay Ward, one of very few production houses actually in the geographical area called Hollywood. Diagonally across an intersection (what Americans call 'kitty-corner from here') is the site of the old Schwab's drugstore, where, according to myth, Lana Turner was discovered drinking a soda by a talent scout, and which was described as 'a combination office, coffee klatch and waiting room' for movie people in the film *Sunset Boulevard.* These days it's a cinema complex, where, I was told, Kevin Costner took his kids to *The Secret of Roan Inish* and Peter Berg took Juliette Lewis to see *The Last Seduction*, just a few days before my visit. (People tell you things like this all the time in Los Angeles, although you never see celebrities with your own eyes.)

Go left a couple of blocks from the Marmont and you cross Courtney Avenue, where Hugh Grant enacted his own *Pretty Woman* fantasy in 1995. Go right a couple of blocks and you reach a health food restaurant called The Source, where Alvy Singer (Woody Allen) tried to persuade Annie Hall (Dianne Keaton) to come back to him. Keep walking for five minutes, and you'll see the impeccably art deco Argyle Hotel (formerly the St James Club) where Griffin Mill (Tim Robbins) hoped to meet his blackmailer in *The Player*, and where instead he heard a movie pitch by the swimming pool. So many stars have used the Argyle for afternoon liaisons over the years that the locals will tell you 'it used to be a skyscraper, but it got fucked flat'.

A little further along Sunset gets you to a restaurant called Le Dome, where directors and producers go to be seen making deals (as in *Get Shorty*), and then to Johnny Depp's Viper club, where River Phoenix died of a drug overdose in 1993. You're now in the Strip, named after a similar area in Las Vegas, where until 1984 brothels and gambling clubs were legal—or at least not policed. Nowadays tame strip clubs and comedy stores have replaced them. As the Strip stops, Beverly Hills begins, and you'll have to get back in your car.

Sunset Boulevard leads ultimately to the Pacific Ocean, where America ends. If you crave accommodation that has a beach attached, Santa Monica offers the quaint Shangri-La Hotel, built to resemble a 1920s ocean liner, with porthole windows. It's alleged to be a haven for actors, but the only face I've ever recognised there was Donovan Leitch, the 60s folkie/hippie singer of *Sunshine Superman*. It's across the road from a wide grey beach on which, it seems, all the homeless people of America come to sleep, and an amusement pier which provided the merry-go-round in *The Sting* and the scene of the final confrontations in *Ruthless People* and *Falling Down*.

Of course, everything I've said here is based on my

way of viewing LA through the lens of my favourite films. You could construct a completely different city from your own encounters with Hollywoodland. And if you never go to the movies, you'll agree with Raymond Chandler's summation of LA: 'a city with no more personality than a paper cup'.

9 · ISLANDS

Islands are the most attractive of all destinations for two reasons: (1) they embody the idea of escape from life on the mainland, and therefore the freedom to throw aside rules and inhibitions; and (2) being small and circumscribed by water, they give the illusion that it is possible to comprehend them, perhaps even conquer them, and the excuse to keep exploring until you have succeeded.

The three islands in the world which best illustrate these attractions are, in increasing order of sophistication, Erakor, Hydra and Capri. Here's why.

Capri

When I think of Capri, I think of lemons. I am having dinner in a lemon orchard attached to a restaurant called Da Paolino. Electric light bulbs are hanging from the trees. I've had pasta with preserved lemons, fish with lemon sauce, and lemon delicious pudding, and now, with my coffee, I'm drinking a sweet yellow liqueur called Limoncello. My dinner companion, who was born on Capri and tries to return here once a year, is telling me the island has the perfect soil and climate for growing lemons, oranges, olives, grapes, figs and artichokes. The fertility was what attracted people to the island in the first place, but now, my companion complains, there are so many people there's hardly space to plant anything. After all, the place is only six kilometres long and three kilometres wide, and on some days in peak season, 100,000 people are trying to fit onto it.

Guidebooks often say that Capri gets its name from *capri*, the Latin word for goats, which used to abound there. But there's an equally good chance the name came from *kapros*, the Greek word for wild boar, which the Greeks used to hunt on the island several hundred years before the Romans arrived. Either way, the only goats and boars on Capri these days are bustling off the ferries from Naples and Sorrento and cramming into the fashion shops around Piazza Umberto. The miracle of Capri is that it has survived 2000 years of such visitors without losing a drop of its spectacular charm. It testifies to the power of island-ness.

The Roman emperor Tiberius built a retirement palace at one end of the island in 27 AD and lived there for his last ten years, throwing his boyfriends off the cliff when they ceased to amuse him. The writer Axel Munthe built a mansion at the other end of the island in the 1880s, collecting Roman statuary and planting a gorgeous garden. Between those sites, it would be easy to dismiss Capri as a clutter of flash hotels, overpriced restaurants and tacky discotheques, but when you get away from the glitz (strolling to the ruins of Tiberius's Villa Iovis, for example, or taking the chairlift over the orchards to

Munthe's Villa San Michele at Anacapri) and you look down the cliffs to the turquoise ocean, you can see why Capri will still be a place of intrigue and escape in another 2000 years.

Hydra

A roaring smelly hydrofoil takes 90 minutes to bounce you from Athens to Hydra (pronounced eedra). I suspect the ride is a clever psychological trick to make you appreciate the island's silence all the more. Hydra's port is surrounded by about 2000 red-roofed houses, rising into the hills like seats in an amphitheatre, with the harbour as the stage. Some of them are whitewashed cottages. Some of them are elegant mansions. Most of them are empty.

As you clamber up the cobbled lanes, you pass shuttered windows and collapsed balconies more often than you pass open doorways. Two centuries ago 30,000 rich and influential people lived on Hydra. Nowadays the population is less than 3000, and most of them survive by goatherding and fishing, or by serving terrible food and overpriced trinkets to daytrippers. Glorious Hydra, whose sailors once ruled the Mediterranean, is now a shopping stopover for the cruise-boat industry. But a few minutes from the port, it is something else:

'Islands are places of mystery. Washed by the greater mysteries of wind and sea, swept over by tides of human events, they accumulate eerie magnetisms that attract the lawless, the eccentric, and—it is said—the supernatural; they shelter oddments of civilisation that evolve into involute societies, and their histories are less likely to reflect orderly patterns of culture than mosaics of bizarre circumstance.'

That comment came from *A Traveller's Tale* by Lucius Shepherd, published in *Isaac Asimov's Science Fiction*

Magazine in 1984. The story was fiction, but the passage could describe Hydra and the phrase 'mosaics of bizarre circumstance' perfectly sums up its history. The name means 'watering place'—a funny description for the barren rocky landscape you see today. But 3000 years ago Greek seafarers would stop here for fresh water and a walk in the pine forests. Now the springs have dried up and the trees have been chopped down.

The island stayed untouched until the 16th century, when it became a refuge for people fleeing the warfare between the Venetian Empire and the Ottoman Empire. In terms of modern geography, the settlers were a mixture of Turks, Italians, Greeks and Albanians. They started building ships to trade with neighbouring islands, and they weren't above a bit of piracy. By the mid-18th century the Hydriotes were the most successful merchant mariners of the region. Although nominally under the control of Ottoman Turkey, Hydra functioned as an independent city-state, happily trading with the Russians, who were supposedly at war with the Ottomans.

The islanders made their biggest profits during the Napoleonic Wars, when the British were blockading French possessions. The tough navigators from Hydra were able to run the blockade, bringing wheat and other supplies to France and returning home with four times the value of their original investments. This was the golden age, when the ship captains built themselves extravagant mansions on the hills around Hydra's port, while the sailors built themselves comfortable cottages.

In the 1820s a group of intellectuals on the mainland began calling for a revolution to overthrow the Ottoman rulers and make Greece an independent nation. The Hydriotes belatedly joined the struggle and waged a successful guerilla campaign against the much larger

Ottoman navy, culminating in a decisive victory in 1827. It is no exaggeration to say the sailors of Hydra won Greece its freedom.

But in fighting the revolution, Hydra spent its fortune and lost its market. With Europe at peace, there were no more blockades to run. When other fleets began to convert to steam in the mid-19th century, Hydra couldn't afford to. Its sailors were recruited for the navies of other nations. By the early 20th century farming and sponge fishing were the island's only industries. In the 1950s Hydra became an artists' colony where English intellectuals seeking 'creative freedom' moved into the empty houses and wrote about each other, painted each other, and slept with each other. Among them were the Australian writers Charmian Clift and George Johnston.

All these fragments of the mosaic are traceable as you walk into the hills away from the harbour front. The island is 23 kilometres long and six kilometres wide, so it's easy to find emptiness beyond the farms and monasteries and goats. There are no cars, except for a three-wheeled garbage truck. The usual mode of transport is donkey. There are no pretty beaches—if you want to swim, you must jump off rocks into cold, green depths.

Hydra's appeal is not really explainable on rational grounds. After a couple of days, you're scared by how strongly you want to stay forever.

Erakor

Vanuatu is a South Pacific nation made up entirely of islands—83 of them, although the nation's 160,000 citizens mostly live on the 11 biggest ones. Its smallest inhabited island is Erakor, which translates as 'safe within the fence'.

At the time of my visit, in mid-1992, Vanuatu was

going through exciting times. Control of the government had recently shifted from an English-speaking political party to a French-speaking party. There were questions about whether Vanuatu would retain its status as a tax haven. The Australian High Commissioner had just been expelled because he had implied that the Finance Minister was corrupt. And the locals were out in the streets of the capital, Port Vila, celebrating two momentous events: the introduction of television, and 12 years of independence from joint British and French rule (an 80-year administration that was officially known as The Condominium of the New Hebrides, but locally known as 'the pandemonium').

The atmosphere was as turbulent as it ever gets amongst people whose perpetually placid manner no doubt results from spending their lives on islands. There were banners on the office blocks in three languages—English, French and a pidgin English called Bislama. A band was playing outside the main electrical goods shop, which had two TV sets in its window (showing the Olympic Games). At night there were fireworks and crowds in the bars that specialise in a muddy drink called kava (made from the roots of a pepper plant). Port Vila felt too much like a mainland. It was time to escape.

Within an hour I could have been on an island with a live volcano, or an island of cargo cultists who worship an American soldier they call John From, or an island where bungee jumping with vines was invented hundreds of years ago as an initiation ceremony for teenage boys. But instead I chose Erakor, because it seemed to offer the essence of island-ness. Getting there requires a 20-minute bus ride from the centre of Port Vila, followed by a five-minute boat ride. You step off the little ferry onto a rainforest-covered coral atoll about three kilometres long and half a kilometre wide, ringed by sand. Amongst the trees there are eight small bungalows and one restaurant, which served a very satisfying crab with chilli and coconut sauce on the night of our arrival.

Next morning my friend and I were woken at 6am by roosters crowing and dogs barking on a nearby island. We got up, stepped out of our door directly onto the beach, and watched the peak-hour traffic—six people vigorously rowing towards us, then dragging their outrigger canoes onto the sand and entering the restaurant block to set up breakfast. The island's tribal owners haven't lived on Erakor since 1959, when it was devastated by a hurricane. They moved their village to the next island, which is less attractive although more sheltered. But they don't mind popping over each morning to service their investment in visitors who are foolish enough to risk the wind.

The word idyllic is no exaggeration for Erakor. The restaurant manager will lend you goggles and snorkel so you can swim in the lagoon and examine clumps of pink coral while tiny blue and yellow fish nibble your fingertips. At one end of the island you can watch the locals catching the fish for lunch (theirs and yours). They drape nets over long sticks they have stuck into the seabed and then splash through the water, driving the fish into the nets. In the middle of the island there's a ruined longhouse where the tribe used to meet, and the outline of a church which has lost its roof and most of its walls. Walking through the forest and round the beaches takes about an hour. Then you're obliged to relax. In the unlikely event that you want to leave the island, you go to one end of the beach and rattle a stick in a bucket hanging from a tree. A sign above the bucket offers this instruction: 'Sippos you want ferry, you killim gong'.

Somehow the ferryman, wherever he may be, hears the sound and putt-putts up to the beach within ten minutes.

After a couple of days of swimming and eating I started to feel my usual compulsion to justify the journey with scholarship. I asked in the restaurant if anyone could tell me about the history of the island. Oh yes, they said, it has all been written down by a local historian named M. Totar. They handed me a single roneoed sheet. 'The name was given by the ANCESTORS,' M. Totar writes, referring to the arrival of the first inhabitants about 2000 years ago. 'Erakor is like a rock, became a shelter, where people can hide due to tribal wars, welcomed different colours of people with their custom cultures. A place where many missionaries witnessed that there is hospitality. One of them exclaimed Erakor "the village of peace".'

'It was not until late 1959 a few days after Christmas when the people of Erakor were celebrating (which came to be the last Christmas celebrated at this beautiful little island) and were already in the mood of expecting a very happy new year 1960 when the hurricane struck the island. The island was left empty except for a few goats, fowls, cats etc. Later on the island started to grow bush, weeds, shrubs etc and nobody ever wanted to touch it. [Later] the first Australian businessman won the community's approval of establishing a tourist resort. The clearings begun and the buildings erected and it officially opened in 1980.'

I gained another impression of local history the next day when I was walking in the forest and came upon five gravestones. Three of them are whitewashed and bear no names. The other two reveal a tale of struggle. The one on the left says: 'Thy will be done. In Memory of Joseph A, who died Dec 25th 1875, aged 13 months. Arthur, who died Sept 27th 1878, aged 19 months. Walter B, who died Feb 12th 1887, aged 19 months. Beloved children of J. W. and Amanda MacKenzie'. The one on the right says: 'Erected by the New Hebrides Missionaries. In Loving Memory of Amanda Bruce, wife of Rev J. W. MacKenzie. Who died at Erakor 30th April 1893 after 21 years Christian work … Her last words were "I know that Jesus is mine and I am His".' Amanda MacKenzie gave birth to three children and watched them die, thousands of miles from her homeland, but stayed on to carry out her Christian duty. That's what islands can do to your mind.

10 · JERUSALEM

If this book is about the power of place—how certain environments can inspire ideas, passions and transformations—then Jerusalem is the most powerful place on the planet. It is the only place that has a form of madness named after it. The Jerusalem Syndrome is a disorder that afflicts some people after they have been in the city for a few days. They start thinking they are Jesus Christ, or the Virgin Mary or King David or even Satan. The doctor who named the syndrome in 1982, Yair Bar El, treats the sufferers at the Kfar Shaul psychiatric hospital on Jerusalem's northwestern outskirts. He says about 80 percent of the pilgrims who develop delusions of divinity have a history of psychological disturbance before they come to Jerusalem. The other 20 percent are normal visitors who just seem to snap under the historical and religious weight of the city; most of them are Protestants.

An article on the syndrome in *The Atlantic Monthly* magazine in 1995 noted that it often strikes travellers when they are in the wilderness outside Jerusalem. 'Members of the Israeli army, should they find a European or an American wandering in bed sheets, looking for locusts and wild honey, know to take him to Kfar Shaul . . . If Jesus came again to Jerusalem, this is perhaps where he'd be taken'.

A typical case, *The Atlantic Monthly* reported, was a computer programmer from New York City who visited Jerusalem in June 1994 and began to suspect he might be Jesus. But then, he couldn't decide what to do about it. 'In the medieval world, his path would have been clearer,' the article said. 'He could have gathered some followers and thrust himself into the Divine limelight. In the modern world, however, divinity like his, once so integral to the life and history of the church, is now anachronistic, its purpose phased out long ago.' Back in New York after treatment at Kfar Shaul, he was embarrassed about his delusion and afraid to return to Jerusalem in case it happened again.

Yair Bar El has treated hundreds of messiahs and prophets and holy virgins. 'The most important thing,' he says, 'is to get them away from the stimulus. Once away from the city, they are usually fine.' That's the power of place.

But I am puzzled how the psychiatrists can so easily distinguish between symptoms they label as mad and the belief systems that inspire most of the pilgrims to Jerusalem. The reasons for the city's importance to three of the great religions of the world do not sound to me like the essence of rationality:

(1) The idea that it is possible to communicate with God by placing letters or faxes between the stones of a wall built near a temple that was destroyed 2000 years ago, combined with the idea that God expects you to wail

near the wall to express regret about the temple's destruction.

(2) The idea that a person described as 'the Son of God' was crucified by Roman invaders 2000 years ago and buried at a spot that happened to be directly above where the original human being, Adam, was buried.

(3) The belief that a prophet visiting Jerusalem in the 7th century AD was taken bodily up to heaven by the angel Gabriel, spent a night in conversation with God, and returned to communicate what he was told to the rest of humanity.

Number one is what orthodox Jews believe; two is what traditional Christians believe; three is what fundamentalist Muslims believe. Depending on your own faith, you might find one or more of these propositions a little eccentric. But they explain why Jerusalem matters so much to three of the great religions of the world. The Jews say it is the capital of Israel. The Arabs say it is the capital of Palestine. And the Christians say they don't mind whose capital it is as long as nobody touches the Church of the Holy Sepulchre, supposedly built on the spot where Jesus was crucified.

Here are the key points in the history of Jerusalem, as those three faiths would tell it. The city was established as the capital of the Jewish faith in the 10th century BC by King David (some years after he made his name by slaying Goliath). David had been carrying around with him the Ark of the Covenant, a large wooden box which contained, written on stone tablets, the basic laws by which human beings should live. God had given the tablets to Moses 400 years earlier. David built his palace on a hill called Zion, and kept the Ark there. If you have seen the film *Raiders of the Lost Ark*, you will know the Ark's significance. Not only can it emit laser beams which

burn the flesh off Nazis, but it symbolises the special rela-
tionship between God and the Israelites.

David's son Solomon built a temple to house the Ark
on a hill which came to be called Temple Mount, but in
the 6th century BC the temple was destroyed by invading
forces, and the Ark disappeared. When the Jews regained
control of Jerusalem, a new temple was built on the
mount, but this was destroyed by the Romans in 70 AD.
The retaining wall on the western side of the temple still
stands. It is thought to be the closest existing spot to
where the Ark was kept. These days it is called the Wailing
Wall, because men in black suits and black hats go there
to bemoan the destruction of the temples (and leave messages for God).

A prophet named Jesus, who was said to be the Son
of God, was crucified by the Romans in Jerusalem around
33 AD. Jesus carried his own cross along a street which is
now called Via Dolorosa (or Al Mujahdeen Road if you're
a Muslim). That event inspired an offshoot of Judaism
called Christianity, a movement which spread rapidly
through Europe. In the 4th century AD the mother of
the Roman emperor Constantine visited Jerusalem and
identified one particular hill as Golgotha, the spot where
Jesus had been crucified and buried. Constantine built a
church there, which has been falling down and rising up
ever since, growing ever more cluttered with chapels
operated by different sects.

In the 7th century a prophet named Mohammed
travelled to Jerusalem from Mecca, stood on the hill
which contained the ruins of the Jewish temple, and was
lifted up for a meeting with God. After Mohammed's
death, his followers took control of Jerusalem and dedicated the Temple Mount to his memory, building elaborate shrines called The Dome of the Rock and the

al-Aqsa Mosque. Initially they tolerated the Jews and the Christians in Jerusalem, but in the 10th century more hardline Moslems from Egypt and Turkey took control of the city and made it difficult for other faiths to worship there. European Christians were outraged, and organised the Crusades, a series of military campaigns which led to the capture of Jerusalem in 1099.

The Arabs got it back 90 years later but allowed religious freedom to Jews and Christians. The city stayed in the control of the Ottoman Turks until the 20th century, then was taken over by the British during World War I. Britain administered it until 1948, when the State of Israel was established. As part of the bargaining between Britain, Israel and the surrounding Arab countries, Jerusalem was divided, with the eastern half (including the part within the old walls) under the control of Jordan, and the western half controlled by Israel. During the Six-Day War with the Arab countries in 1967, Israel took over the whole of Jerusalem and declared it to be the nation's capital, despite condemnation by the United Nations.

These days the eastern half is still mainly inhabited by Arabs, who regularly protest against Israeli control. If you stay in a hotel called the American Colony (which, despite its name, was once a Muslim caliph's palace) you'll be in the midst of the Arab quarter, and you'll be woken regularly at night by loudspeakers in the nearby mosque intoning 'Allah is great, there is no God but Allah, and Mohammed is His prophet'.

Part of the explanation for Jerusalem's hypnotic influence for 3000 bloody years must lie in the physical beauty of its setting and its graceful honey-coloured buildings. Back in 1869, the author Mark Twain led a party of rich Americans on a package tour of the world. In his account of the journey, *The Innocents Abroad*, Twain described their approach to Jerusalem:

'Perched on its eternal hills, white and domed and solid, massed together and hooped with high grey walls, the venerable city gleamed in the sun. So small! Why, it was no larger than an American village of four thousand inhabitants, and no larger than an ordinary Syrian city of thirty thousand. Jerusalem numbers only fourteen thousand people. We dismounted and looked, without speaking a dozen sentences, across the wide intervening valley for an hour or more ... Tears would have been out of place. The thoughts Jerusalem suggests are full of poetry, sublimity, and, more than all, dignity.'

Nowadays, if Twain were trying to stand on that hill to look at the old city, he'd be run over by earthmoving equipment. Apartments and office blocks are going up at a frenzied pace, as the Israelis stake their claim to the territory they seized in 1967. The new buildings are monumentally ugly. The population within the old walls is now 30,000, with another half a million people clustered just outside them.

Inside the old city, Twain gave this description: 'The streets are roughly and badly paved with stone, and are tolerably crooked ... Lepers, cripples, the blind and the idiotic assail you on every hand, and they know but one word of but one language apparently—baksheesh.' Baksheesh is the Arab term for a monetary gift. The experience of walking in Jerusalem is the same today, except that the lepers have been replaced by relentless youths claiming to be students and offering to act as guides to the city. Twain had no shortage of such guides, one of whom showed him Adam's grave within the Holy Sepulchre. Twain was moved: 'How touching it was, here in a land of strangers, far away from home and friends and all who cared for me, thus to discover the grave of a blood relation. I leaned upon a pillar and burst into tears. Noble old man—he did not live to see me, he did not live to see his child. Weighed down by sorrow and disappointment, he died before I was born—six thousand brief summers before I was born'. We can safely assume that Twain was in no danger of suffering The Jerusalem Syndrome.

Travellers whose faith is of a more secular kind prefer to exercise their emotions in the Israel Museum, which celebrates the achievements of Jews all over the world. It contains the original manuscript of Albert Einstein's Theory of Relativity, written in 1912 (the earliest of Einstein's scientific papers in existence). On one page it looks as if Einstein originally wrote his famous formula for the conversion of mass into energy as $L=MC^2$, then crossed out the L and replaced it with E. The assumption is that the L might have been the Greek letter *lambda*, which was sometimes used to stand for energy.

Einstein complained in his later years that some people were trying to turn him into a 'Jewish saint', and that's exactly what has happened at the Israel Museum. But what else would you expect in this city? I am sure that in years to come, there will be pilgrims to Jerusalem who will be admitted to Kfar Shaul hospital because they are convinced they are the reincarnations of Albert Einstein.

11 · KOWLOON, CHINA

Bruce Lee, the kung fu movie star, knew the meaning of the word Kowloon, so he had only himself to blame when he died of a brain haemorrhage at the age of 32. In Cantonese, *gau* means nine and *loong* means dragon. Kowloon, which is at the tip of mainland China, got the name long ago because there were hills behind it that looked like the backs of eight dragons (the ninth dragon was the Emperor who decided upon the name). The area kept the name when it was ceded to the British in 1861 after The Second Opium War (which started, like The First Opium War, because China was trying to stop British traders from selling opium to the Chinese). So Kowloon is part of the place we now call Hong Kong (along with Hong Kong Island, which Britain won from China in The First Opium War in 1841, and an area called The New Territories, which Britain leased from China for 99 years back in 1898).

All that historical stuff matters much less than the

significance of the name, about which Bruce Lee had been warned when he moved into the fashionable suburb of Kowloon Tong in 1973. At 32, he had not yet learned humility. He was told that the villa he wanted to buy had bad fung shui. Lee's name in Cantonese was Shao-loong, which means 'little dragon'. Naturally the nine dragons would be angry if another dragon settled in to challenge their supremacy. Apart from which, Kowloon Tong is in a valley, which is bad for the flow of positive energies.

Lee was sceptical, but just in case, he called in a geomancer, who advised him that if he hung an eight-sided mirror called a bhat gwa outside his front door, he might be able to deflect the negative energies. Then while Lee was away in Hollywood, a typhoon blew the mirror down, leaving him at the mercy of the dragons. And so he died.

This story is often repeated in Hong Kong as a warning to westerners about mucking around with cosmic forces. The Chinese of Hong Kong will tell you straightforwardly that they have two obsessions: money and food. They are very good at making both. They will announce proudly that Hong Kong has the world's highest proportion of millionaires among its population, and the world's highest rate of Rolls-Royce ownership and cognac consumption. If you ask the secret of their success, they can give you the answer in two words: fung shui. Pronounced either foong shoy or foong shway, it translates literally as 'wind water', and it means the art of creating harmony between human beings and their environment.

Fung shui combines geography, astronomy, astrology, meteorology, architecture, psychology, mythology and even paronomasia (punning on words with similar sounds). Narrowly interpreted, it guides the design of buildings and the placement of furniture. But broadly interpreted by an expert, at the right price, fung shui can guarantee wealth, health and happiness. For the visitor, it explains why so many things in Hong Kong look strange.

There are little eight-sided mirrors on walls and windows all over the city. In hotels, pictures often hang at an angle, and if you try to straighten them, someone will come along to tilt them again. That's so bad luck will slide off. Doors into restaurants often open onto a wall or a screen, and you'll have to make a sudden left or right turn to get inside. That's to confuse the bad spirits, and to make it harder for the money inside to fly out.

Enter an office and you'll have to look around for its inhabitant; a fundamental of fung shui is that a desk must never face a door. The same applies to your bed at home. And of course, there won't be a roof beam running lengthwise over the middle of the bed, because that signifies the likely separation of the couple who sleep there. There'll be no tree anywhere near the front door of the house because that would inhibit the incoming flow of energy. The front and back doors will not be in a straight line because the energy could flow straight out again. If the house or office doesn't look onto water, there'll be an aquarium in the main room, or if that isn't practical, a picture of water on the wall, because the flow of water symbolises the flow of money.

There'll be a lot of gold and red in the colour schemes because they symbolise joy and festivity, unless there is a need to encourage meditation, in which case there'll be a lot of blue. There'll be no grey or black, which mean disaster and grief. If the house or office is open plan, there will be plants, aquariums, screens and mirrors strategically placed to hold the useful energy ('bandaids against bad fung shui', as one geomancer described them). And no sensible person would be living at the end of a cul de sac, because the street would focus negative energy into the house.

In the 1980s, a new apartment complex in the wealthy Hong Kong suburb of Repulse Bay was built with a massive square hole in the middle. That was to provide water access for the dragon who lives on the hill behind the bay. (Since the block is blue and the hole is outlined in orange, it's been hailed as a spectacular example of postmodernist architecture.) For a similar reason, the ground floor of the Regent Hotel on the Kowloon shoreline has plate glass front and back—the dragons would be angry at having their harbour access blocked if the walls were brick.

The architect I. M. Pei paid no attention to the rules of fung shui when commissioned by the mainland Chinese government to design the Bank of China building in Hong Kong in the early 1980s. The communists disapprove of superstitions, and anyway Pei has his own concept of harmony. There was an outcry when it became apparent that the sharp angles of the new skyscraper would direct beams of bad luck directly at Government House, which had previously enjoyed good fung shui with its commanding water views. Was it a communist plot to undermine the British administration? Government House sought the advice of a geomancer and set up bhat gwa mirrors at particular angles on its balcony to send the bad luck in harmless directions.

The system called fung shui originated in ancient Chinese theories about the way the universe works, which were formalised in the 12th century by a scholar called Wang Chi. He wrote that everything started with a force called *ch'i*, 'the breath of nature'. The first things that flowed from ch'i were the male principle, yang, and the female principle, yin, followed by the rest of the universe, which operates on a strict set of laws designed to balance yang and yin. The geomancer interprets these laws and offers humans some ways to take advantage of them.

The laws of the universe are not necessarily fair. In March of 1993, I was discussing the Bruce Lee story with Chong Hon, a Hong Kong-trained geomancer who now makes a lot of money advising the Chinese community in Sydney about buying and furnishing homes. He remarked that once bad fung shui has affected a family, it can continue through the next three generations. That's just the way it is. Two weeks after our conversation, Bruce Lee's son Brandon, who was making a film in Hollywood called *The Crow*, was killed in an accident with a gun on the set. Hong Kong people would say he had not done enough to lift the curse that struck his father.

In Hong Kong I met the Australian boss of a small publishing company who had just moved into a new suite of offices. One of his senior staff had suggested using fung shui to determine the placement of furniture. The geomancer studied the plans, measured the area with a special set of compasses and rulers, drew up a set of numbers on a grid that looked like a noughts and crosses game, investigated weather patterns and local beliefs about dragons and spirits, and interviewed every employee, noting in particular their birth dates.

Then she suggested moving the front door six inches to the right and repainting the walls to remove all green. She put strips of tape on the carpet to show where the desks should go. She was unhappy with the atmosphere of the intended conference room, and advised that either its walls should be knocked down or it should be kept locked and never used. When the workers finally moved in (on the date judged auspicious), the geomancer burned incense in the corners and arranged the serving of a barbecued pig. And as she left, she reminded the boss that whenever the employees changed, she would need to return and rebalance the equation.

So it turned into an expensive exercise. There is no official scale of fees for geomancers, but the company boss got the hint that a gift of about 5000 Hong Kong dollars would be appropriate. Plus, of course, all the renovations. He considered it an investment in staff morale. I asked if he actually believed the application of fung shui would ensure his financial success. 'I don't know,' he said, 'but why take chances?' (He knew anyway that few Chinese would do business with him if they found out his offices had not been fung shui-approved.)

At least he didn't have to undertake the kind of major replanning forced on the British when they proposed building a telegraph line between Hong Kong and Canton early this century. In this case the bad fung shui was based on the symbolism of place names rather than geography. Guangzhou (Canton) translates as 'city of sheep'. The part of the river through which the telegraph line was supposed to pass was called 'tiger's mouth'. The line was due to end up in Kowloon. So the citizens of Canton visualised a rope that would pull the sheep through a tiger's mouth and thence into the lair of nine dragons. A lot of geomancers earned a lot of money working out ways to save those sheep from a painful fate.

Worrying about the shape of things and the meaning of places is only the start of your search for success in Hong Kong. You'd better know about wordplay too. The Cantonese word for 'eight' sounds like the word for 'rich'. It's just a pun, but it explains why a businessman paid five million Hong Kong dollars for a licence plate with nothing but 8 on it. It's the equivalent of an English-speaking gambler always betting on number one because it sounds like 'won'. The Hong Kong administration regularly auctions significant licence numbers and phone numbers, and donates the proceeds to charity. People who miss out on eights are happy to settle for three, which sounds like 'born', or nine, which sounds like 'eternity'. And when I tell you that 1988 was a year of great rejoicing in Hong Kong, you will realise that it was not in honour of Australia's bicentenary. You may imagine how much money was invested at Hong Kong's two racecourses on August the eighth of that year.

There's a power station in the suburb of Aberdeen which has five chimneys. It needs only four, but the word for 'four' sounds like 'die' in Cantonese, and that is just asking for trouble in a power station, so the designers incorporated an extra chimney. On the same principle, many buildings in Hong Kong do not have a fourth floor or a fourteenth floor. A newlywed couple whose name in Cantonese meant 'twin trees' were advised to move away from an area with a lot of English speakers, because the English mispronounced their name to sound like 'twin corpses'.

So you've moved house, redesigned your doors and furniture, hung your mirrors, bought an aquarium, and anticipated all meanings and puns on the names in your life. But what have you done for your ancestors? To ensure they are comfortable in the afterlife you'd better buy paper models of a house, servants, mobile phone, VCR, tape deck and Mercedes Benz to burn next to their grave. (The complete kit of paper possessions costs 80 Hong Kong dollars, a price designed to make them even luckier.) And you'll want a little altar in your house, crowded with images of your favourite ancestors, within which you can burn red paper to appease your kitchen god.

While I was visiting a temple with a Hong Kong friend, I asked a foolish question: 'What actual religion are these people practising?' He smiled and said it was Buddhism, Taoism, Confucianism, animism and a bunch of other theories that have no particular label. Every family tailors its own mixture according to what it has found to be successful. Every profession or trade has a special god that watches over it—for example Tin Hau, the goddess of seafarers, Wong Tai Sin, who represents healers, and Kwan Tai, whose image is in every police station and, oddly enough, every brothel in Hong Kong. The faithful know that most of these gods are stupid, and can be bribed cheaply with gifts of food and fake money. The more rituals you follow, the greater your chance of happening upon the right one.

The best temple in which to observe the complex belief system of Hong Kong is on top of Lantau Island, about 70 minutes by ferry from Hong Kong's central harbour. After a terrifying ten-minute bus ride up narrow winding roads, you're very grateful for the peace of Po-Lin ('precious lotus') Monastery. Theoretically the faith being practised there is Buddhist, which is indicated by the world's biggest outdoor statue of Buddha sitting nearby. It looks oddly feminine, despite being 34 metres tall and made of 248 tonnes of bronze. Inside the temple there are fierce-looking golden gods being appeased by bowls of fruit, joss sticks are filling the place with overpowering scents, and what appear to be bonbons are hanging from the ceiling. You can pay a fortune teller to burn incense for you and interpret the pattern of the bamboo sticks you have shaken up and thrown from a box called a *chim*.

But the real treat is the vegetarian lunch the monks at the monastery will cook for you. First a thick soup of noodles, spinach and bean curd, then spring rolls, and then a fragrant stew containing five types of mushroom, each with a different flavour and texture, on a bed of corn, peas and seaweed. If vegetarian food were always like this, the world would give up meat in a minute. The food, the fresh air and the forest walks around the temple may tempt those who have become oppressed by the intensity of Hong Kong to stay on Lantau Peak for a few days. The monks will charge you 150 Hong Kong dollars a night to sleep in the monastery. But be warned: they start beating drums and clanging gongs at 5am. That's also part of ensuring your future is happy and profitable.

A few years ago, a journalist annoyed the actress Shirley Maclaine by asking her: 'Is there anything you *don't* believe in?' If you put that question to most of the citizens of Hong Kong, they would smile and reply: 'Just one thing: taking any risks'.

12 · LOCARNO, SWITZERLAND

The most spectacular one-day journey you can make in Europe ends at Locarno, and after it, the town may seem like an anti-climax. You could easily conclude that Locarno is the sort of place where Obsessive Traveller's Rule Number One might have to be applied: when you find yourself in a strange town with nothing to do, and you've already taken care of your laundry, head for the local graveyard. The odds are you'll learn something about human nature. Locarno proved the worth of that rule, and the town turned out to have more to offer than simple proximity to some tantalising tombs. But let us begin with the journey.

After a few days in the capital of German-speaking Switzerland (see Chapter 26) I was curious to see how different the atmosphere might be in the Italian-speaking part of the country. On the face of it, the term 'Italian Swiss' seemed as much of an oxymoron as 'army intelligence'. It was hard to imagine how Swiss precision could ever marry with Italian hedonism. I chose Locarno for my research when I learned that it's where the German Swiss go for their honeymoons, a resort town offering fun in the sun combined with the security of staying within the fatherland. And if there's one thing the Swiss value, it's security.

To reach Locarno, I discovered, it's necessary to slide down the spine of Switzerland, using a combination of boat and train that is called The William Tell Express. The first stage is a 40-minute train ride from Zurich to Lucerne, where you board a large launch for a three-hour glide along a body of water which the English call Lake Lucerne and which the Swiss call the Lake of the Four Cantons. You need to allow at least an hour to look round Lucerne, primarily to walk over the Chapel Bridge, built in 1333. It is covered with a wooden roof whose eaves are thick with cobwebs—a sign of good luck, say the Swiss. The activities of William Tell are frequent among the scenes painted on the ceiling, because William Tell is the biggest thing that ever happened—or never happened— to this area.

The boat leaves at 11.25 a.m., as scheduled, and the first sacred site it passes on the left is the Grand Hotel Nationale, where César Ritz and Auguste Escoffier began a partnership in 1877 that changed the history of hospitality (see Chapter 18). A little further to the left, at the tip of a spur in the lake, is the village of Kussnacht, where Ritz died insane in a private clinic in 1918. The boat served a lunch that would not be the envy of Escoffier in a vaguely art deco dining room at 11.45 a.m., as scheduled. I ate vegetable soup, salty veal stew with little green dumplings called *spaetzle*, and a chocolate ice cream with the William Tell insignia branded into it. The Italian part of Switzerland couldn't come soon enough for me.

In the introduction to this book I promised that I would not be writing about scenery. I must make an exception for the panorama that greeted me when I emerged on deck from the dining room. The cow-studded, mist-draped, snow-capped green slopes on both sides of the lake make chocolate box paintings look black and white. Icarus-like figures hang glide from the tops of these hills, and swans slide round the bottom of them.

You could comfortably spend the next two hours just gaping at all this, but then you'd miss the bits of the journey that reveal more about the Swiss psyche. The boat pulls into a landing platform called Rutli, from which a flight of steps leads to the most important patch of grass in Swiss history. In 1291, three tribal groups whose territory bordered the lake met on Rutli meadow and agreed to form a mutual defence pact against foreign aggression (which at the time meant Austria). That union became a nation called Switzerland, and those communities became the first three cantons (there are now 23). In 1859, when the private owners of the meadow announced they were planning to build a hotel on it, a bunch of Swiss patriots organised a fund-raising campaign, mainly among schoolchildren, to buy the meadow and preserve it for the nation. The meadow stirs tremendous emotion in the normally placid Swiss, and early in World War II, the head of the Swiss Army, General Henri Guisan, plucked that heartstring to prevent the country splitting into pro-German and pro-Allied cantons. He organised a rally at Rutli meadow where military officers from every canton gathered to repeat the original oath and declare their allegiance to Swiss unity and neutrality.

Next the boat passes a site called Tell's Rock. I'd better tell you the story. The year is 1307. The Austrians are in control of the area. A hunter called Wilhelm Tell and his son are passing through a town called Altdorf when soldiers tell them they have to bow their heads to a hat on a stick to show their loyalty to an Austrian Governor named Gessler (his first name is never mentioned). Tell refuses, gets arrested, and Gessler says the only way to save the life of his son is for Tell to shoot an apple off the boy's head with his crossbow. Tell takes two arrows from his quiver, puts one in his belt and the other in the bow, and shoots the apple through the middle. Gessler asks what the other arrow is for, and Tell says it was for Gessler if the boy had been hurt. Tell is arrested again and the soldiers take him in a boat across the lake to incarcerate him in a dungeon. Up comes a storm and the soldiers plead with Tell (an expert sailor as well as marksman) to steer the boat to safety. He does so, but as the boat nears land, Tell jumps out onto a rock and runs off into the forest. Later he ambushes and kills Gessler near the village of Kussnacht, starting an uprising that frees Switzerland from Austrian tyranny. So now we are looking at the actual rock onto which Tell jumped to make his escape. Is any of this true? The answer is in Chapter 26.

Our boat docks at Fluellen, where a boy with a sign on a stick leads the passengers to a comfortable modern train which leaves one minute early at 3.14 p.m. Almost immediately we pass through Altdorf, which now has a statue of Tell to commemorate the hat and apple incident. Then we start climbing. We are about to experience a miracle of engineering. Between 1872 and 1880 some 3000 engineers with a lot of dynamite blasted a hole through the Gotthard mountain range and connected German Switzerland with Italian Switzerland. In the process, 30 of them died. Now the train crawls over fragile bridges and twists through tunnels in the shape of corkscrews and horseshoes to climb to 1100 metres above sea level and back down again. At the village of Wassen, we have the bizarre experience of approaching the same little white church three times as the train enters and leaves a series of tunnels that spiral round the town. Finally, after ten minutes in the darkness of the Gotthard Tunnel, we emerge in Ticino, which has been part of Switzerland since the year 1500, but where the Swiss speak Italian.

The difference is immediately apparent in the colouring of the buildings, which are orange, while German Switzerland tends to be white. We start to see grapevines, cornfields and chestnut trees, and suddenly the railway platforms bear signs like *uscita* and *binario*, instead of *ausgang* and *steig*. I find this very comforting, but I'm puzzled, when I finally leave the train at Locarno, to see the decidedly non-Italian word FART writ large on several signs. This is not a token gesture for German speakers. I learn that it's the initials of the canton's public transport service—Ferrovia Autolinea Regionale Ticinese.

The place to stay in Locarno for devotees of seediness is undoubtedly the Grand Hotel, which embodies faded glory. When it opened in 1870, with the world's biggest Murano glass chandelier suspended through three floors above its lobby, it was meant to grow fat on Switzerland's tourist boom, especially once the train tunnel through the mountains was blasted out. But as early as 1876, when César Ritz became the maitre d' of its restaurant, things were starting to go wrong at The Grand. The manager would have given Basil Fawlty a run for his money. Living on a diet of raw ham, bread and a great deal of wine, he was constantly confused by the process of assigning guests to their rooms and delivering their luggage. He seemed to exist in a different time zone from other humans, liking to ring the dinner bell at 5am.

On one occasion he chased his supposedly unfaithful wife through the corridors, shooting at her with his army pistol. Ritz noted in his memoirs: 'I did what I could to pacify the clients'. Nowadays the chandelier is still hanging, but life at the Grand is less dramatic. My room has creaking floors, a mattress which feels as if it was installed in 1870, and a shower on a stick connected to the bath taps by a rubber hose. But the plump mono-grammed towels cry out to be souvenired.

When I take my first stroll, I find that Locarno is clean and pretty, like northern Swiss towns, but, unlike them, it is warm (averaging 2286 hours of sunshine a year, com-pared with Zurich's 1693). Camellias are blooming every-where, joined by magnolias and palm trees in the parks that stretch along Lake Maggiore. The people strolling seem mostly to be over 60, although there are a few young groov-ers mucking about in boats. Locarno (population 17,000, growing to 50,000 in peak season) looks like the sort of place where the citizens in the graveyard would be more interesting than the ones walking around.

Which leads me to the tale of Christophe Orelli. Strictly speaking, Christophe Orelli is not in a graveyard. He had himself buried under the entrance to Locarno's Church of St Francis. Indeed, his gravestone forms the front step. He did this for revenge on his fellow citizens, according to Claus Muller, a local history buff who was showing me around. I thought it seemed an odd sort of revenge, to be trodden on by everyone who enters the church. 'Ah,' said Muller, 'there's the story.'

Orelli was a rich middle-aged man who made the mistake of fancying a 16-year-old girl and of being reluc-tant to marry her, in a small town in the south of Swit-zerland in the middle of the 17th century. It was not a time or a place to offend conventional morality. The locals made his life hell (proving, said Muller, that even that long ago the citizens of Locarno were more Swiss than Italian). When the young woman moved into his mansion, Orelli found himself under siege. People spat at him in the street and no-one would sell him food. Seeking a way to recover the goodwill of his fellow citizens, he took the advice of a local bishop and built a magnificent baroque church with cherubs crawling all over the ceiling. By the time of his death he'd used up his fortune but regained his food deliveries.

Naturally the locals expected he'd honour their community by being buried in the Church of the Assumption he had built for them. But Orelli was damned if he was going to suck up to his neighbours for eternity. He chose instead to honour a competing church in an adjoining community, rejoicing in a final act of snubbing the people who had snubbed him. His much eroded gravestone at the door of St Francis Church is engraved with a request to leave the soul of 'poor Orelli' to its rest.

It seems that people in Locarno have funny ideas about their posthumous powers. Claus Muller drove me to a cemetery about 20 kilometres south of town at the top of a hill overlooking Lake Maggiore (remarking during the journey that the worst drivers on the road were tourists from Italy). The cemetery contains the remains of Max Emden, who made a fortune from copper mining in the early 20th century and retired to his own island in the middle of the lake, building a Roman-style villa there. According to Muller, Emden surrounded himself with 40 beautiful women, and everyone on the island walked around naked. When he felt time's winged chariot at his heel, Emden bought a gravesite at Ronco Sopra Ascona, which would allow him a view of his island. But then someone pointed out that his corpse would be lying on its back and therefore unable to look down to the desired spot. His solution was to have a column built above the grave, topped with a sculpture of his head, so that it formed a kind of periscope through which his corpse could check the doings on his property.

When you go grave hunting, there are always bonuses. Muller pointed to an adjoining tomb and commented that it belonged to Erich Maria Remarque, whom he described as 'the author of *Nothing New On The Western Front*'. Next to Remarque was the actress Paulette Goddard, who had married Remarque after his book was made into a film. It was the same kind of incidental discovery I had enjoyed in the Swiss town of Vevey, when I was seeking the grave of Charlie Chaplin and came upon the simple wooden cross of Graham Greene.

Claus Muller is a bit of a gravewatcher, like me, but that's not the main reason he enjoys living in Locarno. Its charm, he says, is that it's 'like a watch with Swiss clockwork in an Italian-designed case'. As we wandered through crowded cobbled streets that could have been anywhere in northern Italy, Muller pointed to a large metal cube beside the road and said: 'That's our air pollution monitoring system. As soon as the pollution gets above a certain level, we close this part of town to cars'. Such sensible planning would be impossible any further south.

At lunch in a restaurant called Trattoria da Luigi, we ate *crostini* laden with porcini mushrooms and garlic, and a fabulous antipasto that included duck breast, squid, artichoke and local mozzarella cheese. We drank a local red wine called merlot. It felt comfortably Italian. The waiters began clearing away the antipasto table at 1.45, and by 2.15, we were the only customers left. Everyone had returned to work, Muller explained, noting with approval that Locarno had long ago dispensed with the time-wasting idea of siesta.

When my pasta arrived, I asked for a pepper grinder, and the waiter went in search of one. Muller was curious. 'You want to grind pepper on your pasta, do you? The Italians always do that. And will you want to put a lot of olive oil on your salad?' I nodded. He became reflective: 'This is interesting. I think you Australians must be more like the Italians than you are like the Swiss.' I refrained from saying that I found this a great compliment.

13 · MIAMI, USA

Along Ocean Drive at South Miami Beach, brown-skinned glossy men and alarmingly thin women sit on the balconies of renovated art deco hotels, nibbling at pasta and sipping on multicoloured cocktails from which project tiny umbrellas and plastic animals. The men are trying to pick up the women, or each other. The women are waiting to be discovered as models—'between photo shoots', as they say. But this layer of glamour, which has been the city's image ever since *Miami Vice*, is thinner than the models' makeup. Just three blocks inland, on Washington Avenue, you're back in America's deep south, and the poor white south at that.

In the middle of a row of dusty shops with window displays that seem not to have changed since 1956, you'll find Lulu's Bar, where the beer is served in jam jars and today's special on the menu is a peanut butter and banana sandwich fried in chicken fat. What's so special about that? 'It was Elvis's favourite food,' explains the lady at the bar, and suggests I might like to take a look upstairs before I order my lunch.

Upstairs is a room overflowing with everything Elvis—posters, luminous paintings on black velvet, plastic statues, record covers, salt shakers, guitars, ashtrays and countless photographs. Back downstairs I tell the bar lady I enjoyed her Elvis museum. 'Oh, it's not really a museum,' she says modestly, 'it's just a shrine.' She serves me corn and okra fritters with maple syrup, peppery chicken gumbo with dirty rice (which has mashed giblets stirred through it) and very sweet apple pie with ice cream. It's enough to feed any of those beachfront models for a month, except of course that they wouldn't be seen dead at Lulu's.

Yet Lulu's does not represent 'the real Miami' any more than the postmodern cafes on Ocean Drive. Miami is not a town of either poor white trash or rich white trash. To find the real Miami, you have to go a lot further inland. And you need to know that when you get there, English will be the second language.

Cross the causeway that connects the long thin strip of Miami Beach to the mainland (detouring right to see the mansion on Palm Island where Al Capone died of syphilis in 1947), and head west into the business district. If you're worried about Miami's reputation for violence, make sure you use only the expressway turnoffs marked with a small drawing of a palm tree. The palm signs mean the exits are police patrolled, giving tourists some assurance that they won't fall victim to gangs who bump into the backs of cars and rob the occupants when they get out to investigate.

But be reassured that the tourist murder rate is minimal compared with the rate at which Miamians kill each other. In the early 80s Miami was honoured with the title 'Murder Capital of the USA' because the rate topped 600 a year. The central morgue ran out of space and had to rent a refrigerated truck from Burger King to hold the surplus corpses. The city authorities got the message and invested $12 million to build the most technologically advanced morgue in the world: The Joseph H. Davis Center for Forensic Pathology, located on Bob Hope Road. It can handle 350 murder victims at a time, and to avoid unfortunate mixups, the corpses are computer barcoded.

The violence wave has settled down a bit lately as the city's drug gangs reached understandings about their turfs. What is apparent now is that there are mountains of money around the town waiting to be spent. Miami has more banks per head of population than any US city. So where is the money going? Into a building boom, producing spectacular skyscrapers and sprawling shopping centres.

This unchecked development so alarmed Carl Hiassen, a columnist with *The Miami Herald*, that he embarked on a series of satirical novels which portray Miami as a polluted hellhole: *Tourist Season, Double Whammy, Native Tongue* and *Strip Tease*. I asked him if his plan was to destroy the tourist industry. 'Not destroy it,' he said, 'but cripple it. I don't mind tourists at all—it's the people who stay who worry me. Any biologist or naturalist or anyone that's ever studied any species will tell you that if you crowd too many people into too small an area, first they use up the resources and then they start killing each other. We're well into phase two of that now, and as someone who was born and raised here, it's a little distressing to see the sheer numbers of people and not know how their children or their grandchildren are going to make it. My aim is not to terrify, just to put them on alert. The humour in the books is so obvious that reading the daily newspaper is much more terrifying down here.'

Hiassen says some of his readers think he must be 'on drugs' to produce the scenarios in his novels, but nothing he invents can match the absurdity of Florida's reality. He offers these examples:

- In 1992, during a meeting of the local Crimewatch citizens group in the town of Homestead, just outside Miami, a 75-pound bale of cocaine fell from an aeroplane and landed in the middle of the meeting.

- As the result of an application from certain people in Florida, the US Supreme Court is considering whether animal sacrifice should be considered a legal religious practice in the US. 'One time my son went fishing and came back with a headless chicken wrapped in men's boxer shorts,' Hiassen recalls. 'I don't know what kind of a curse that is, but somebody's real pissed off.'

- The home of the head of the Miami Chamber of Commerce was burgled. Police reported that the main item stolen was an Uzi submachine gun from under the bed.

Of course, Hiassen has to admit that all the things he hates about modern Miami make it the perfect place to set thrillers—whether in the form of novels, or movies such as *Miami Blues*, or TV series such as *Miami Vice*. And this is no doubt why so many of America's most successful pulp fictioneers now live there. Edna Buchanan, who worked as Chief Crime Reporter on *The Miami Herald* for 20 years, has now retired from journalism to produce novels. She estimates that in her career she reported on 5000 violent deaths, of which 3000 were murders and hundreds remain unsolved. At least in novels such as *Contents Under Pressure* and *Miami, It's Murder*, she can ensure that justice is done (usually by the intervention of her heroine, Britt Montero, who is, oddly enough, a crime reporter for a Miami daily paper).

Buchanan lists the attractions of Miami for her as 'drug smuggling, money laundering, mass murder, the Mafia, deposed dictators, foreign fugitives, cocaine cowboys, street people, terrorists, bombings, grave robbings, bizarre sects, bizarre sex, animal sacrifice, voodoo, gun running, vast wealth, utter poverty, crazy politics, racial tensions, refugees and riots'. But she offers this advice to visitors: 'The majority of murder victims who wind up at the morgue contribute to their own demise. They deal drugs, steal, rob or stray with someone else's mate. They are impolite in traffic or skirmish over parking spaces with other motorists who happen to be well armed and short tempered. The average murder victim is not an average citizen. Most have arrest records and drugs, alcohol or both aboard when shot down. Solid citizens who stay alert are usually safe'.

Another novelist, James Hall, who lives just south of Miami and finds it a constant inspiration for twisted plots and violent characters, says Florida has always been weird, but only in the mid-80s did that weirdness become fashionable. He says 20th century history in Florida can be divided into three periods: Before *Miami Vice* (BMV), During *Miami Vice* (DMV), and After *Miami Vice* (AMV).

'Before *Miami Vice*, Florida virtually did not exist,' he says. 'It was the place your grandmother went to retire, the place you'd only visit if you were really desperate for rubber alligators and garish t-shirts, this strange exotic place that really did not belong to America. Then there was the DMV period. All of us, whether we care to admit it or not, owe a great debt to Don Johnson. He gave us unconstructed jackets and lavender t-shirts and Phil Collins rock music in the background. That period brought Florida onto the national stage in a way that had never been possible before. Now we are in this difficult period AMV, when we have to figure out what is true, we have to find out how to investigate this region and explore and mine its unique quirkiness and beauty and glamour without ruining it.'

Drive through the business district along Brickell Avenue and you'll see an example of the DMV legacy: an apartment complex with a pyramid on top and a huge square hole in the middle which contains a spiral staircase going nowhere. The building appeared in the opening scenes of *Miami Vice* and it is typical of the work of Miami's hottest design firm, Arquitectonica. According to Beth Dunlop, architecture critic for *The Miami Herald*, Miami is about to replace Chicago as the great design laboratory of America, blending its past fads of art deco, Hollywood Spanish, and high tech into a style unique in the world.

I asked Dunlop why so much of Miami was painted pink and green. 'This is a place that looks good in colours,' she said. 'The sky is very low and bright blue, the clouds are very big, but it doesn't have topography. It has the water and it has the land, and white sunlight, but it's all flat, no vantage points. When you look out at Miami, what you see is colour.

'Pink and green were the fashionable colours here in the 50s, and in the 80s the producer of *Miami Vice*, Michael Mann, came in and issued a three-word edict to his designers and to the people choosing his locations— no earth tones. So when *Miami Vice* showed Miami how splendid it could look, life imitated art. Suddenly everything started getting painted up. It was like a fireworks display—the easiest thing to do with your building was to paint the outside. You didn't have to renovate the interior, but you'd be on TV and you could finally sell it or rent it.'

But the DMV architectural fantasies along Brickell Avenue don't represent the real Miami any more than the hedonism of the beachfront. Head north into the suburbs, and look around at the single-storey cottages squashed together, and the rows of peeling shops with signs in Spanish. Now you're getting closer to reality. Of the four million people who live in greater Miami, three million are of Hispanic origin. Sociologists often call Miami 'the city of the future' because it previews the makeup of most big American cities by the year 2030, when Anglo-Saxons will be in a minority and their traditions will no longer be taken for granted. That makes it an essential place for anyone who expects to be travelling in the 21st century.

Miami may be the most southern city in the United States, but it would be more accurate to describe it as the most northern city of Latin America. And the wealthiest. Not only do Miami's banks hold the funds of Latin America's dictators, drug lords and land barons, but some of the people who arrived here as refugees from poverty have done very well for themselves.

Many of the richest recent arrivals live in a suburb called Coral Gables, and this represents a considerable irony. Coral Gables was developed in the 1920s by an entrepreneur named George Merrick, who dreamed of turning swampy land on the edge of the Everglades into 'America's Riviera'. His architects were told to draw their inspiration from Spain, particularly the Alhambra Palace in Granada, and Merrick named the streets after localities around the Mediterranean. When he ran out of real names, Merrick simply made up names that sounded suitably Spanish. Of course, the intended buyers of his real estate were Americans of Anglo origin. No-one in that era imagined that wealthy customers might appear from

South America. Long after his death, Merrick's 'City Beautiful' is finally inhabited by people who actually speak the language of its streets.

Which brings us to a restaurant in Coral Gables called Yuca, a classic symbol of the new Miami. The name is a pun. A yuca is a South American root vegetable, but the initials also stand for Miami's version of the Yuppie: 'Young Upscale Cuban-American'. Nobody these days would dream of naming a restaurant 'Yuppie', with its stigma of 80s arrogance, but Miami's Yucas love to advertise their success, and happily cram into the two-storey, white-walled and neon-decorated restaurant named after them (even if their land of origin wasn't Cuba).

In fact, Yuca is one of the most interesting eateries I've experienced anywhere. Latin American food in Miami usually means variations on a dish called *pollo asado*, sometimes called *arroz con pollo*, which is chicken stewed in onions and sage, sitting on white rice, surrounded with black beans simmered in pork fat and topped with slices of fried banana. Yuca doesn't serve pollo asado. Yuca's chicken comes with a sauce of tamarind and pasilla peppers, sitting on white beans and saffron potatoes. Its black beans come pureed in a luscious soup dotted with rice cakes. Its bananas are in a spiced lentil sauce served with grilled swordfish, oyster croquettes and aioli, or in a coconut rice pudding with passionfruit sauce. There is even yuca root itself, tasting a bit like parsnip and mingled with cabbage and mint in a salad served with lamb chops.

To deal with Yuca, you'll need to know that if you order *Filete de rabirubia soasado con comino y semillas de calabaza con salsa de mamey y naranja, servido con pure de papas poblano*, you'll get a fish called yellowtail, coated with cumin and pumpkin seeds, served on potatoes mashed with poblano peppers and covered with a blood orange sauce. And if you order *Terrina de ciruelas y peras frescas, salsa de natilla de canela y salsa de ciruelas*, you'll get a terrine of plums and pears, with a cinnamon custard sauce and a plum sauce. This is not peasant food. Yuca's dishes are monuments to conspicuous consumption.

You don't have to be a fan of *Miami Vice* to get the most out of Miami, and you don't have to bring a bullet-proof vest to survive. But to understand The City of the Future, you will certainly need to learn Spanish. And remember not to ask where the money comes from.

14 · NOOSA, AUSTRALIA

Not that I take holidays, of course, but if I had to define the ideal spot for a week's holiday, I'd begin by requiring it to have five adventurous restaurants (not six, because you like to return to the best one on your last night). Then I'd say: one good bookshop, lots of bushland within walking distance, a clean beach, a room with a view and room service, two cinemas, a baby-sitting service, reliable public transport, and five eccentric sights within a short bus or train ride.

It's a dream. But on that scale, Noosa scores nine out of ten. The best goat stew with chickpeas I've ever eaten was just the first of many surprises. Then there was the experience of walking down Hastings Street after dinner to discover that the pavement cafes had flickering candles beneath their umbrellas, so that the whole block glowed with golden light and conversation, blending with the breeze through the trees and the whoosh of the ocean.

Instead of the mini Miami I had been dreading, the Noosans have somehow managed to put together a combination of inner-city sophistication, resort comfort and untouched nature—Santa Monica without the squalor, St Tropez without the snobbery, a tropical rainforest with good coffee.

I'd arrived grudgingly and grumpily, having explained to my wife that Travel is for the purpose of learning about other cultures, and there was nothing we could learn by sitting on the sand in Queensland for seven days. I was not much cheered by her observation that I would be travelling to Australia's most peculiar state, famed for political and police corruption, with the highest suicide rate on the mainland (14.2 per 100,000 compared with a national figure of 12.6) and the highest rate of attempted murder (4.4 per 100,000 compared with a national figure of 1.9).

She tried another tack. 'This is not Travel,' she said. 'This is A Holiday, which is a different thing. You shouldn't need to take your notebook out at any stage.' She held the pessimistic view that having a two-year-old child meant that Travel was denied to us for the moment, so we would have to substitute the word 'relaxing' for 'interesting' in our holiday aspirations. As it turned out, Noosa was too much of the latter to be much of the former. I had my notebook out all the time. Queensland's Sunshine Coast contains both the finest and the funniest manifestations of Australia's current obsession with tourism.

The nation whose economy used to be summed up in the cliche 'Australia rides on the sheep's back' is now clinging to the shoulders of the three million strangers who fly in every year. We still sell wool, wheat and minerals to the world, but none of them comes near the billions we make each year from selling The Australian

Experience to foreigners. Yet we don't believe our country has enough natural charms to keep the visitors amused. We feel compelled to manufacture attractions. Small entrepreneurs are convinced that if they set up an Object of Interest in a vaguely scenic area, the dollars, yens and pounds will fly in the door. The subject matter for these fabrications varies from the absurd to the pathetic, but I wouldn't want to lose a single one of them.

Australia already had a great history of silliness in its national monuments, as evidenced by the 'Bigs' that dot the countryside. Whenever I travel in Australia, I'll always detour to see a Big, and my collection so far includes The Big Lobster, the Big Banana, The Big Potato, the Big Merino, the Big Prawn, the Big Lawn Mower, the Big Ned Kelly and The Big Soap.

Now that these sites have an international audience, the tourism entrepreneurs have drawn on this rich tradition to create more elaborate enticements. And Queensland's Sunshine Coast has the greatest concentration of Fabricated Attractions in the land. Forget about the Great Barrier Reef and the rainforests and the mountains. The following more meaningful experiences can be found within 30 kilometres of Noosa: The Big Pineapple, the Big Shell (and hattery), The Big Pelican, the House of Bottles, the Ginger Factory (including Koala Kottage and Granny's Macadamia Kitchen), the Super Bee (including the Bellingham Maze), the Bli Bli Medieval Castle, Teddy Bear Land, the Big Kart Track (Australia's biggest), the Forest Glen Deer Sanctuary, the Endeavour Replica, the Queensland Reptile Park, and Aussie World (including the Ettamogah Pub and the Motorcycle Museum).

Transcending them all is Nostalgia Town, just next to the Sunshine Freeway at Maroochydore. Our party of three adults and two children arrived at 11am to find Nostalgia Town apparently deserted. There was no-one at the ticket counter, so we wandered into a vast barn crammed with shopping opportunities. Finally we discovered a couple of ladies taking tea in the Nostalgia Town Cafe. They seemed surprised to see us, since it was between tour bus visits, but one of them agreed to sell us tickets to the Enchanted Railway and Albert's Incredible Time Trip.

The miniature railway takes a 750-metre-long circuit past a series of ponds, near which papier mâché dinosaurs and neanderthals can be glimpsed peeping out of undergrowth. I couldn't help wondering at the meaning of the word 'nostalgia' in this context. I'd always thought it referred to fond memories of earlier experiences, and it seemed unlikely many visitors to Nostalgia Town would have spent their childhood in the Mesozoic period. Perhaps we were being nostalgic about the day we went to see *Jurassic Park* at the cinema.

We got off the train and were mucking around on the Graveyard Putt (a mini-golf obstacle course through tombstones) when the ticket seller bustled out and warned us we'd better hurry or we'd miss Albert's Incredible Time Trip. Just because we were the only customers there, they weren't about to be diverted from their admirably strict timetable. We boarded another train and were towed past a series of tableaux from Australian history, linked by recurring characters called Ben Tooter, Buck Teaf and Ian O'Sent. Initially they appeared as convicts fighting a giant snake as they made their escape. We then saw their descendants at the gold rush, patronising a laundry run by a Chinese figure identified as No Pong. Finally they appeared as local election candidates (sharing a ticket with M. Bitious, Richa Backhander, R.

U. Gulible, and U. Greasemepalm). As we passed a room in which they were addressing a council meeting, we saw a dark-suited figure outside, carrying a briefcase labelled 'Fitzgerald Inquiry'—a reference to the investigation in the late 1980s which uncovered massive corruption among Queensland police and politicians.

What on earth would the Japanese bus party who were entering Nostalgia Town as we departed make of all that? But Nostalgia Town must be doing something right, because its brochures say proudly 'Winners of consecutive Sunshine Coast Tourism Awards, 1993 and 1994—Best Significant Local Attraction'.

Could it be the presence of all these Big Wonder Theme Park World Lands that is causing the current population explosion in Queensland? Its birth rate may be below the replacement level, but it gains 50,000 permanent residents a year, while all other states are either static or declining in population. And the wealthiest of those 50,000 new arrivals seem to settle on the Sunshine Coast, judging by the gorgeous canal developments being lined with mansions and boat moorings.

I prefer to think that the newcomers are drawn to Noosa by its status as the food capital of Australia. Numerically there may be more good restaurants in Sydney or Melbourne, but for its size, Noosa has the nation's highest concentration of imaginative eateries, along with a hinterland of farms growing exotic fruits, herbs and vegetables that until recently had to be imported from Thailand.

A typical glutton's day in paradise might begin with breakfast of banana pancakes with maple syrup or potato blinis with salmon while contemplating the surf at Eduardo's On the Beach. Lunch might be taken at Saltwater, which is upstairs on a patio overlooking Hastings Street, with polished wooden chairs that could have come off an ocean liner. It does light spicy seafood and the best takeaway fish and chips (and octopus and scallops and tempura vegies) in the nation.

Across the road is your dinner destination—La Plage, which stretches onto the pavement and offers French colonial dishes of a kind you wish they'd serve in New Caledonia, including the aforementioned Moroccan stew of milk-fed kid with chickpeas, okra, zucchini and capsicum in a clay pot. In the unlikely event that you tire of repeated visits to Saltwater and La Plage, you could try the trendy Aqua Bar, which has multicoloured cocktails and describes its food as 'lite moderne' (Caesar salad, tempura prawns, onion and walnut tart).

When the glutton is ready to venture from the security of Hastings Street, a boardwalk over a hill leads to Coco's on the edge of the rainforest, which has a Swiss owner and a menu influenced by China and Japan.

A 45-minute launch ride along the Noosa River ends at a comfortable homestead restaurant called The Jetty at Boreen Point. It's on a tree-covered spit of land where, according to a plaque, a convict named Dennis rescued a castaway named Eliza Fraser in 1836. There's no menu, and you must take what the chefs want to give you. In our case it was a five-course Greek feast, including filo pastry stuffed with spinach and ricotta, and slabs of tender lamb.

A 20-minute drive south from Noosa gets you to The Spirit House at Yandina, serving Thai food in the prettiest setting I've encountered in an Australian restaurant— under hanging plants, beside a lake, each table surrounded by shrubs. Have I reached five adventurous restaurants already? But I hadn't mentioned Filligan's at Munna Point, or Chilli Jam Thai at Noosaville!

Those for whom food is less of a preoccupation might spend more time in the National Park, which happens to be 20 minutes' walk from Hastings Street. They can plunge into winding trails through dense rain-forests, encountering fat goannas sunning themselves across the path, and emerge after a couple of hours at deserted rocky beaches.

Or they might take a magical mystery tour from the end of Hastings Street on the local bus marked either Tewantin or Sunshine Beach (it's the same one, going round and round). In the Sunshine Beach direction they could study the architectural extravaganzas built by the new settlers. In the other direction they'd pass national treasures such as the home of the tennis champion Evonne Goolagong, The Big Shell (crammed with the world's greatest concentration of kitsch souvenirs) and The House of Bottles (built, says a sign, by George Clifford, who was the first human being to successfully put coloured sands in a bottle).

At the Tewantin end they might get off and catch a punt across a river to a camel sanctuary. The bus driver advised against this: 'You wouldn't get me on them, dirty smelly things'. (We made the cross-river trek later in a four-wheel drive, bypassing the camel rides, and zoomed for two hours along a beach to the red and yellow sand-hills where George Clifford did that first historic bottle fill. We also climbed inside the rusting hulk of a cargo ship that was cast ashore in a storm during the 1970s and could never be refloated.)

So let's add it up: Noosa has two small but useful bookshops; a coffee bar with so many permutations of cream, marshmallow, vanilla and cinnamon that it should be in Seattle; a three-screen cinema five minutes' drive away at Noosa Junction; and a reliable baby-sitting service.

And yes, our room, at a place called Seahaven, had a 180-degree view of the clean beach, plus a barbecue apparatus on the balcony, revolving ceiling-fans, a jacuzzi, and room service provided by a neighbouring Italian restaurant.

But it was still only A Holiday. If the Noosans could just bring themselves to speak a foreign language, I could call it Travel, and go back again.

15 · ORVIETO, ITALY

There's a fabulous zebra-striped cathedral at one end of the Piazza del Duomo in Orvieto—a gothic masterpiece built between 1290 and 1600 with a facade that includes technicolour mosaics, gargoyles, balconies and a rose window—but that was not what was holding my attention as I stood in the middle of the square. I was concentrating on a cart displaying hundreds of white and yellow porcelain jugs in the shape of roosters, each with the word 'Orvieto' baked into the glazed surface just under the beak. I was confronting the classic dilemma for travellers who don't want to be tourists: should I actually buy a souvenir?

Certainly there was a lot worth remembering about Orvieto, starting with the local white wine made from grapes grown in the volcanic soil at the base of the huge rock on which the town stands (the dry version being a lot better than the sweet *abbocato* version). There's a medieval maze of tiny lanes winding between terracotta-roofed houses made of the same brown volcanic rock. And there's a weird well, built in the 1530s at the order of Pope Clement the Seventh, who had taken refuge behind Orvieto's high walls after French troops sacked Rome, and who wanted to guarantee a water supply. The Pozzo di San Patrizio project turned into a miracle of engineering, with two spiral staircases, each of 248 steps, winding around the shaft but never meeting. One staircase was for donkeys to go down, and the other was for them to bring the water up. Undertaking the downward climb and the upward return leaves you with trembling thighs and a sense that you've earned another serving of porchetta (roast wild pig that, ideally, has fed on wild fennel in the forest, or at least has been flavoured with it).

A souvenir of Orvieto would also symbolise the general superiority of Umbrian hill towns over their more fashionable Tuscan counterparts. In Umbria, a hill is really a hill (or, in the case of Orvieto, a volcanic tufa). Once you've developed an inclination for Orvieto, you inevitably move up to Gubbio and Assisi. In Assisi you can escape the tour buses surrounding the cathedral by doing a leisurely one-hour climb to the rock where Saint Francis preached to the animals. Having thus honed his communication skills, Francis went on to do a miracle in Gubbio some time around 1220, which involved persuading a wolf to stop attacking the townsfolk. The local restaurant named after that event—Taverna del Lupo— serves a wonderful soup called *imbrecciata*, thick with beans, corn, lentils, peas and celery. The menu says it's from a 'Eugubian' recipe, which presumably means it was eaten by the ancient Romans when the town was called Eugubium (although it's unlikely that back then the soup included corn, which only arrived in Italy in the 16th century, after Columbus found it in South America).

Gubbio is as steep as you could want an Umbrian hill town to be, but you can cheat by taking a rattly little funicular up to the basilica which contains the mummified corpse of Saint Ubaldo, who fought off various barbarians in 1155. He's in a glass coffin above the altar, and has a tan that George Hamilton would envy and cheekbones worthy of Faye Dunaway. Unfortunately Ubaldo's mouth dropped open some time in the last 800 years, and no-one has had the nerve to reach in and close it.

In the basilica you can also see the three *ceri*, which are wooden pillars used in the annual festival of Ubaldo. On 15 May each year, huge wax figures of saints Ubaldo, Anthony and George are mounted on top of these pillars, and the totem poles thus created are carried through the streets of Gubbio and up the hill in a race between teams dedicated to each saint.

Once you've seen the saintly mummy, you can wander across to the archaeological diggings, which regularly unearth relics of the Umbri tribe that lived on these hills in the 4th century BC. The Umbri were a placid lot in a period when all the other tribes were warmongers, yet somehow the Umbri managed to persuade the Etruscans not to tear them apart. The image of Umbria as the most peaceful and reflective region of Italy may have grown from this ancient reputation, and certainly towns like Orvieto and Gubbio are famed these days for their quietness. But this may also have something to do with the fact that almost nobody lives in their historic centres any more, except people servicing the tourist industry—sellers of porcelain jugs in the shape of roosters, for example.

Hence my dilemma. I wouldn't have hesitated to spend 5000 lire on that jug, but there were so many roosters on that cart and on the three other carts in the Piazza del Duomo, all displaying the products of the local porcelain factories, that I felt I was at the end point of a massive production line. Still, there was no-one around to call me a tourist, so I did it—checking as best I could to ensure the jugs weren't made in Japan (mine had 'Duomo 12' stamped on the bottom, which was reassuring).

Orvieto became one of my essential places because of the lesson it taught me. When I got back home, I formulated The First Rule of Travel Memorabilia: *a souvenir always looks dumbest when you buy it.* The further you get from the place of purchase, both in space and in time, the more interesting the souvenir will seem. I've decided that you should never be deterred from buying a souvenir by the fear that your friends will call you a nerd, because the more they mock, the more they are secretly jealous. Nowadays I'm very fond of my rooster because: (a) it's useful; (b) it reminds me of a happy journey; (c) it makes my friends say 'where did you get *that?*' and I can reply 'It's written on the front'. If they go on about it too much, I forget to tell them that the wine comes out of the beak rather than out of the top of the jug, and they splash themselves.

Once you've decided that you will be a souvenir collector, you must steel yourself to discard all considerations of good taste. The Second Rule of Travel Memorabilia is: *even the ugliest souvenir is justified if it's functional.* I particularly like mugs and glasses, and my collection includes decorated drinking utensils from the Roy Rogers Museum in Victorville, California (a rearing horse); Exotic World in Helendale, California (a striptease dancer); and the Richard Nixon Museum in Orange County, California (a presidential seal). My baggage is heaviest when I'm returning from California.

At hotels and restaurants, I always take any biros that are marked with the establishment's insignia, and they become my favourite writing implements for weeks afterwards. If the hotel's bidet cloths are similarly emblazoned, I might take a couple of them as well (not that I have a bidet, but, thoroughly washed, they make excellent napkins).

In Italy, I try to eat at restaurants which belong to a society called l'Unione dei Ristoranti del Buon Ricordo, whose members celebrate the unique cooking of their regions (Taverna del Lupo in Gubbio is one of them). Any customer who chooses the chef's favourite dish is rewarded with a terracotta plate that bears a crude illustration of the speciality. I have gathered 29 of these plates over the years, depicting pigeons, prawns, ravioli, cows, squid, pigs, horses and rabbits, and every time I use them they bring back memories of bus, train and foot journeys to obscure villages and suburbs from Brescia to Catania.

The essence of all this is summed up in the Third Rule: *it's the souvenirs you don't collect that you regret later.* Back in 1977, I was obliged to work for eight months in the town of Antwerp, Belgium, and I found myself amid spectacular celebrations of International Rubens Year (the 400th anniversary of the painter's birth). Kitsch was everywhere—Rubens spoons, Rubens beer mugs, Rubens plates, Rubens t-shirts, Rubens wallets, even 'Rubensoep', a mixture of chopped vegetables sold in plastic bags at the markets, supposedly symbolising the colours of his paintings, but actually a way of getting rid of old produce.

I never bought a single item. I was suffering at the time from a kind of snobbery that is totally counter-productive (this was before my epiphany at Orvieto). I thought that, as a resident of the city, I should be above such garish trinkets. I was wrong. Nowadays I'd love to have Rubens on a t-shirt along with my Vanuatu palm trees, my Santa Fe coyote, my Lyme Regis cobb, my Hydra fish, and my Charlie Chaplin silhouette from Vevey, Switzerland (where he is buried). Yes, I have accumulated an extremely vulgar t-shirt collection in my travels, and I wear them all the time.

But if you happen to have a Rubens beer mug, please don't phone and offer it to me. My strict Rule Number Four is: *you can only pick up a souvenir at the time and place where you had the experience.* Once you've missed your chance, you cannot compensate later. No-one else can buy a souvenir *for* you.

I bent that rule a bit when I was in Vienna. A magnificent snowglobe caught my eye, depicting St Stephen's Cathedral and a large ferris wheel (under water, as is the way with snowglobes). At that point I had seen the cathedral but I had not seen the ferris wheel. Was I entitled to buy the snowglobe? I reached this agreement with my conscience—I could buy the snowglobe on the strict understanding that I would go and see the wheel before I left Vienna. I'm glad I did. It turned out to be the world's oldest still-functioning ferris wheel, built in 1897, standing in the Prater amusement park which has served as a recreation area for the Viennese since the 17th century. The gondolas on the wheel are as big as buses, and allow a pleasant view of the flat city when they reach the top. The wheel was used in the film *The Third Man* as the place where Harry Lime met Holly Martens and delivered his analysis of Switzerland (see Chapter 26).

Alright, you're an alert reader and you are now saying that in Vienna I also bent Rule Number Two, since a snowglobe is not strictly functional. True enough, and indeed I am not generally a collector of snowglobes for that reason. In this case, I gave the snowglobe to my mother, who does collect such things, which means I will inherit the Vienna snowglobe one day, along with a whole lot more snowglobes and spoons and ashtrays and paperweights from places I have never been. I will deal with that moral dilemma at the appropriate time.

16 · PRAGUE, THE CZECH
REPUBLIC

If you were standing in the first courtyard of Prague Castle, looking up at the window of President Vaclav Havel's office, and you suddenly saw a body come hurtling through the window, you would, of course, be horrified. But you should not be entirely surprised. If it happened, you would be witnessing the Fifth Great Defenestration of Prague, the latest manifestation of a centuries-old Czech tradition. And for the past 20 years, Vaclav Havel has rejoiced in the title of The Person in Prague Most Likely to be Defenestrated.

Defenestration is the customary method of resolving differences in the land that used to be called Bohemia, and this custom offers the traveller a window into the nature of the society.

Political change in Bohemian culture seems to happen through sudden surges of sentiment followed by real or symbolic defenestrations. Finding the openings through which important people have been thrown is a useful way to organise your exploration of the town with the prettiest face in Europe, now starting to show the first pimples of capitalism. As you move across Prague from the New Town on the southeastern side to the Cernin Palace on the northwestern side, you'll encounter the sites of the four Great Defenestrations of Prague, as well as many near-defenestrations and just plain charming windows.

Before you begin this journey, you need to know the first rule of getting about in Prague: everything in this city is named after Wenceslas. The Czech word for Wenceslas is Vaclav (pronounced vahtslav), so the latest incarnation of the Good King is the President, Vaclav Havel, unless it's the Prime Minister, Vaclav Claus. The king about whom we sing at Christmas—the one who went out in the snow and told a poor man to walk in his footsteps—was not a king at all, just a prince who built a lot of churches when he ruled Bohemia between 921 and 935. Vaclav The Good became a saint after he was murdered by his brother Boleslav The Cruel (stabbed on his way to Mass, probably because there weren't many high windows in Prague at the time). Boleslav stopped building churches and started fighting other tribes until he had expanded Bohemia's territory into what is today the Czech Republic.

The second rule of getting about in Prague is: anything that is not named after King Wenceslas is named after Emperor Charles. The Czech word for Charles is Karol. There were lots of rulers called Charles but the one that matters is Charles IV, who carried out a massive building program in Prague in the mid-14th century. The New Town ('new' meaning built around 1350) is a model of his urban planning.

The First Great Defenestration of Prague happened in 1419, when a bunch of religious reformers invaded the New Town Hall at the end of what is now Charles Square (Karlovo náměstí). They hurled out some town councillors when they refused to release a group of people who had been condemned as heretics. The town hall's main structure was rebuilt last century, so you should look only at the tower if you want to visualise the tumbling bodies. Then walk down a street called Vodičkova, which is Prague's main shopping district, with fabulous art nouveau facades not quite hidden by grime, crowded sausage shops (sausages being the best part of Prague's depressing cuisine), ill-lit stores suddenly crammed with electrical goods and running shoes, and one of the world's biggest McDonald's outlets.

Vodičkova runs into Václavské náměstí (Wenceslas Square) which is really a long thin rectangle. This is where everything happened in post-war Prague: May Day parades after the communist takeover in 1948, the end of the Prague Spring in 1968, the start of the Velvet Revolution in 1989 and the end of communism. At the top of the square there's a statue of Saint Wenceslas, around which the citizens gathered in 1968 when the Soviet tanks rolled in to crush the Czech government's experiment with openness. In 1969 a student named Jan Palach burned himself to death behind the statue, and the locals started lighting candles there as small monuments to the victims of the Soviet invasion.

In November 1989, after months of strikes and demonstrations provoked by the collapse of communism elsewhere in Europe, the police attacked a group of protesting students at the north end of the square and, according to media reports, killed one of the protesters. A million people took to the streets demanding the resignation of the government. The crowd was in a decidedly defenestrating mood, so the communists decided to jump before they were thrown. Then the people in the square started shouting 'Havel to the Castle'. A writer named Vaclav Havel was astonished to find himself leader of a revolution which had, without a gunshot, overthrown a 40-year-old power structure. (A few months later, the protester who had supposedly been killed was found alive and on the payroll of the secret police. The local version of the KGB had apparently organised the street battle as part of its own plan to discredit the regime and replace it with a style of communism similar to Gorbachev's in Moscow. They didn't realise what they were unleashing.)

You can still see the monument to Jan Palach in Wenceslas Square, and on the Narodni Street end there is a banner that says 'zda to se stale', which means 'this is where it happened'—a reference to the police-student battle of 17 November 1989. But otherwise the square no longer has an atmosphere to inspire historical reflection. American residents of Prague (of which there are now many, because they think it is the equivalent of Paris in the 20s) have nicknamed it 'Vacnam', a reference to its likeness to Saigon in the 1960s. It seethes with sightseers, pickpockets, souvenir sellers, hookers, hoods, junkies, cops, con artists and their victims. There are two McDonald's on the square, and in an admirable civic spirit, one store bought a special van for the police to take away drug dealers and thieves.

Go straight ahead out of Wenceslas Square at the opposite end from the statue and you'll soon reach Staroměstské náměstí (Old Town Square), which is really an octagon. The Second Great Defenestration of Prague took place here in 1483—from an upper storey of the Council Chamber. This time the crowd was angry at the execution for heresy of a Catholic reformer called Jan Hus (whose grand monument rises out of the middle of the square), so they dropkicked the mayor and his advisers through their office window.

The Old Town Square is the quaintest meeting place in the world, a multicoloured architectural hodge-podge that Walt Disney would have killed to include in a fairytale. Some tourists stand for an hour waiting for Death and the Apostles to chase each other round the astronomical clock. Nearby, at 9 Bartolomějská Street, you can see where Vaclav Havel was imprisoned and interrogated many times between 1977, when he signed a petition demanding freedom of speech, and the collapse of the government in 1989. These days the political prison has become a backpackers' hostel called Pension Unitas. The metal door of Havel's old cell (room P6) is painted hot pink. Fortunately for Havel, his cell was in the basement.

Next you are on the way to the site of the Third Great Defenestration of Prague, over the river and up the hill to Prague Castle. You must cross by the Charles Bridge (Karlův most).

From childhood I have been a fan of a piece of music called *The Moldau*, written in 1876 by the Czech composer Bedrich Smetana. It perfectly evokes the swirling waters of a river that flows sometimes gently, sometimes fiercely, and it's all the more remarkable when you know that Smetana went deaf shortly before composing it and insane from syphilis shortly afterwards. So my first sighting of a river I knew only by its sound was an emotional moment. The Moldau is wide and dark and a long way below the bridge. I only learned later, with a shock, that it is not actually called the Moldau. It is the Vltava. Moldau was a German word for the river, and if there's one language the Czechs don't want applied to one of their national symbols, it's German.

The Charles Bridge was built in 1400 in honour of the aforementioned Emperor, massively decorated over the centuries, and finally restricted to pedestrian traffic in 1950 (so the communists did one good thing). Nowadays it is lined with 30 smog-blackened statues, countless stalls selling Soviet army caps and badges, lovers keeping rendezvous, painters offering to do your portrait, and buskers singing 1968 rock songs (a Czech obsession because they symbolise the Prague Spring).

The bridge was also the site of what we could think of as a defenestration without a window. In 1383 a priest named John Nepomuk was tied up in a bag and thrown into the river by order of King Wenceslas IV. The story goes that John had refused to tell the king what the queen had said during her confession, so of course he became a saint. There's a tiny figure of John on the metal base of a statue halfway over the bridge on the right-hand side, and you are supposed to rub it for luck, because he's the patron saint of bridge crossers. Given the number of people who crowd onto the bridge every evening—it is the prime target of all 7 million tourists who visit Prague each year—St John's blessing may be the only thing that keeps it from collapsing.

Rapidly passing another McDonald's just over the bridge, you go straight along a street called Mostecká, turn right at the massive baroque Church of Saint Nicholas, then left into Nerudova, and start toiling your way upwards. If this area looks familiar, you must have seen *Amadeus*, because this part of Prague filled in for Vienna in the film. Stop at a rococo pink building on the right-hand side near the top of the street (opposite a staircase). No defenestration happened here, so it's not strictly on your agenda, but Mozart attended a dance here in 1787, on the night he conducted the premiere of *Don Giovanni* in Prague. He would undoubtedly have met Giovanni Casanova at the dance, because the real-life Don Juan was staying in the house at the time, writing his memoirs. Casanova was 62, Mozart was 31.

And finally you reach the top of the hill, and Prague Castle (Pražský hrad), which is not so much a castle as a sprawling complex of chapels, palaces, meeting halls, offices and tiny houses (one of which—22 Golden Lane—was the home of Franz Kafka). The Third Great Defenestration of Prague happened in 1618 from a castle office called the Bohemian Chancellery, which is off the Vladislav Hall (where Vaclav Havel took the presidential oath in December 1989). Once again, the defenestration was the result of a dispute about both religion and politics. A band of Protestant noblemen threw two Catholic governors appointed by the Hapsburg Emperor Ferdinand out of a window straight ahead of you as you enter the second chamber of the Chancellery. When you look out the window, you can see why they survived—it's only about 15 metres from the ground—but one theory at the time was that the Virgin Mary personally parachuted the victims to safety, while other witnesses said they made a soft landing in a dung heap. Either way, the event provoked a 30-year religious war that spread way beyond Bohemia.

About ten minutes' walk to the west of the Castle is the Cernin Palace, a massive ugly block built in 1680 and used in the 20th century as the Czech Ministry of Foreign Affairs. One night in 1948, just after the communists had taken power, the Foreign Minister, Jan Masaryk, went through his office window on the third floor and fell to the paving stones below. The communists, for whom this

Fourth Great Defenestration of Prague was very convenient, said it was suicide. Most people suspected murder, because Masaryk was a local hero (the son of the first President of Czechoslovakia). But in 1990, a search of long-hidden communist files produced a letter written by Masaryk to Joseph Stalin, in which he said he was killing himself as a protest against Stalin's failure to respect Czech independence. It could be a forgery of course, but then, why didn't the communists release it? And Masaryk *was* a manic depressive. Either way, the communists can still be blamed for Masaryk's defenestration, and his spirit must have been smiling when they were forced to jump out of government 40 years later.

Now walk back to Prague Castle and stand in the first courtyard to reflect for a moment on Vaclav Havel's good fortune in not becoming the fifth great defenestratee of Prague. In the first flush of enthusiasm upon becoming president, Havel set about writing a new constitution for Czechoslovakia, organised a free concert by the Rolling Stones, and asked his friend Theodore Pistek, who had won an Oscar for the costumes in *Amadeus*, to design uniforms for the palace guards. Havel was creating a new country as if he was staging a new play. The concert and the costumes went down well—you can see the soldiers in the courtyard strutting proudly in their bright blue blazers with red and white braid and tassels.

The constitution wasn't so widely welcomed. Havel's leftish humanism came up against the Thatcherite conservatism of the new prime minister, Vaclav Claus, and the ambitious opportunism of a former communist named Vladimir Meciar. Meciar, based in the city of Bratislava, took up the cause of Slovak nationalism, blaming the economic troubles of his area on the elitists in Prague. Havel, trying to avoid Yugoslav-style tribal warfare, had to preside over a 'velvet divorce' in which the Slovak nation defenestrated itself.

In December 1992, the nation called Czechoslovakia, which had been patched together from the ruins of the Hapsburg empire in 1918, ceased to exist, and two new countries entered the world—the Czech Republic (population 10 million) and Slovakia (population 5 million). Havel expressed sadness at losing the Slovaks, but given what has happened since, most Czechs think they are well rid of them. The Slovakian Parliament has passed laws allowing Prime Minister Meciar to imprison political opponents who 'destroy sovereignty', 'vilify the nation' or 'spread alarming reports'. The new laws may not actually impose defenestration as the penalty, but it all sounds terribly familiar to those who lived through the 20 years it took for the Prague Spring to finally become summer.

17 · QUILICUM, CANADA

The most horrible thing I have eaten in my adult life is oolican grease. It resembles nothing so much as grey snot, though it is saltier. It was served to me in Quilicum, a restaurant run by people descended from the original inhabitants of an area now called English Bay in Vancouver. As is often the case with food that makes you want to gag on first swallow ('an acquired taste', says the waiter with a slight smile when he sees the reaction of white customers), oolican grease—the melted down fat of a kind of herring—appears on the menu not because it is intended as a gourmet treat, but because it has A Story. It is, in its way, a kind of totem pole.

I went to Quilicum because I'd heard that it served the food of The First Nations, formerly known as the northwestern Indians. I'd found Vancouver a clean and pretty town, but bland in a way that seemed to confirm all the stereotypes I'd been told about Canadians by Americans. Once you've looked for the sites where episodes of *The X-Files* have been filmed (the back streets of Vancouver pose as every American city) there is not a lot to do. Quilicum was my last hope for a surprising experience, although I feared I was going to be trapped in some sort of tourist bubble, with waiters wearing moccasins and feather bonnets—or perhaps, given the local climate, bear furs and snow shoes. It wasn't like that. I descended some wooden stairs into a rectangular room with wooden walls and a pebble floor. A ponytailed young man in jeans and t-shirt showed me to a low bench table made of cedar, where I sat on the floor with my feet in a hole. He suggested a meal of grilled salmon served on a block of wood, caribou stew served in a bowl, and steamed fiddlehead ferns on a plate. The salmon and the caribou were delicious, the fiddleheads were like bitter asparagus.

As a side order, I got bannock bread (originally made from mashed roots but now from wheat) and a pot of oolican grease. After watching me struggle for a while with the condensed phlegm, the waiter remarked that it was a taste I was unlikely to acquire, and that traditionally the northwestern Indians swallowed it in big gulps (bypassing their tastebuds) because it filled their bellies and kept them warm in winter. It occurred to me that for urban Indians eating in a place like Quilicum, the oolican grease might have a nostalgia value not unlike porridge for Anglo-Saxons. But some research showed it meant more than that.

The oolican is a medium-sized silver fish which needs a lot of fat around its bones to keep it warm in the icy waters of the river Nass, which flows through central western Canada. If you put a few hundred oolicans into a big pot and light a fire underneath, pretty soon you'll have a bubbling cauldron of sticky grey goo which lasts virtually forever if you chuck out the bones. For centuries, oolicans have sustained the local tribe called the Nisga'a. The special virtue of the oolican is that it spawns earlier than the salmon, so it always arrived in the Nass Valley in March, when the local residents were on the last of the rations they had saved through the winter. 'When the spring salmon come down the river, the oolican make fun of them, and say, "You guys are too late, we already saved the Nass River people",' says Gordon McKay, of the Nisga'a Tribal Council.

Back in the 1860s, when the representatives of the English queen arrived to take most of the land and force the local people onto reservations, the Nisga'a had to cut down their totem poles, because the Christian missionaries assumed the figures on them were pagan deities. In fact, the totem poles were representations of Nisga'a history, with each carved image serving as a reminder of some past crisis or triumph. It was the equivalent of space aliens arriving in modern Britain and ordering the destruction of all libraries. With the totems gone, the rituals associated with preparing, preserving and consuming oolicans became vital for the continuity of the culture.

Gordon McKay retells, as best he can remember it, his grandfather's explanation of the origin of the oolican, a tale of rescue: 'In the olden days the people had no food and that was when this supernatural man was travelling, called Haimsen. When he was paddling his canoe he saw a seagull diving with a big herring in his mouth. He grabbed the herring away from the seagull, and he made his canoe dive down in the water to where the oolican people live, way down in the bottom of the sea. That's why the oolican came early every year, and that's why our people still survive today'.

For most of the 20th century, the Nisga'a have been fighting to hold onto their traditions and get back their land. The government of British Columbia insisted that their children attend English-speaking schools and 'assimilate' into Canadian culture. Only in the 1980s was there a breakthrough in the form of a court ruling that questioned the legality of the original land division and opened the way for the establishment of schools where the Nisga'a language could be taught alongside English.

Gordon McKay's sister Salome now teaches the younger Nisga'a who live around the Nass River how to make the most of oolicans. The fish that are not rendered down into grease are cut open to remove their guts, and then hung to dry over wooden sticks which go up into the roof beams. Salome McKay thinks oolican grease is the world's most versatile substance: 'We use it on our toast in the morning instead of butter, and for our shortening in baking cakes and hot biscuits. If you have an infection on your body, the grease can heal that. If you have a sunburn, you can rub the grease on your body. You can rub it on your face—that will keep the mosquitoes away from you'. It also represents a modest industry for the people of the Nass River, who package it to send to the small number of First Nations restaurants that have started opening in various Canadian cities.

So Quilicum became an essential place for me because it taught me the value of asking questions, the power of tradition, the importance of persistence and the lesson that food always means more than something to eat.

As I was finishing this book, I phoned Vancouver to check that Quilicum was still going, and learned that it had changed its name to Liliget. Its new owner, Dolly Watt, explained that *quilicum* meant 'gathering place' in a language called Chinook, which was a kind of pidgin Indian imposed by the early English and French invaders to simplify communication with the First Nations. The new name means 'where the people feast' in her own tribal language, Gitskan. (The Gitskan people live on the Skeena River, not far from the Nass Valley.)

Dolly Watt told me that the chef remains the same, and Liliget's menu now features salmon and rabbit grilled over alder branches; venison with wild mushrooms; toasted seaweed; and vegetables such as sweet potatoes and fiddlehead fern shoots. The wine list emphasises the produce of vineyards owned or managed by First Nations people. 'And does Liliget still serve oolican grease?' I asked anxiously. 'Oh yes,' said Dolly Watt. 'We always serve that. But, you know, it's an acquired taste.'

18 · RITZONIA

In his early adult life, César Ritz was an embezzler, and in his late adult life, he was a raving lunatic. But in between times, he was the greatest hotelier the world has ever known. One of the mysteries of history is how the 13th child of a mountain cowherd came to be gifted with an insight into human cravings that would have been envied by Sigmund Freud, and a capacity to translate his insight into physical form that would have been envied by Frank Lloyd Wright.

The actress Lily Langtree, a close friend of King Edward VII of Britain, thought she had part of the explanation: 'Ritz, it is easy to see how you learned tact and patience. You learned those lessons herding your father's stupid cattle in the mountain pastures of the Neiderwald'. The British author C. E. Montague, writing in 1924, also saw significance in Ritz's heritage: 'The Swiss are inspired hotelkeepers. Some centuries since, when a stranger strayed into one of their valleys, their simple forefathers would kill him and share out the little money he might have about him. Now they know better. They keep him alive and writing cheques'.

There were grand hotels in the world before César Ritz, of course. But he turned hotel-making into a science, so that his name entered the language as a synonym for expensive elegance. There are monuments to him everywhere, though they don't always bear his name. When you step through the revolving door of any great hotel, you are entering Ritzonia. And you discover immediately that Ritzonia is another country. They do things differently there.

Wherever I travel, I try to budget to spend two nights in Ritzonia, even if that means crusts and cockroaches for the rest of my journey. If I've paid for my room in a great hotel, nobody can stop me prying into its way of life. I examine every cranny, pad down every mirrored corridor, climb every carpeted staircase, pull the cords, press the buttons and souvenir the symbols. These gilded dinosaurs are essential places for any traveller interested in anthropology, architecture, art, economics, history, psychology and mythology.

Ritz understood that a great hotel has nothing to do with real life or common sense. It is not just a place to sleep, but a destination in itself. Bottles of shampoo, bathrobes and chocolates on your pillow are all very well, but central to a truly great hotel is the fantasy.

Ritz was adamant, for example, that a hotel needed a staircase, because it allowed the guest to Make An Entrance. Your friends have arrived at your hotel to pick you up on the way to the theatre, and they await you in the lobby. You leave your room and sweep down the staircase in your tuxedo or your gown, and all eyes turn to you. This should be one of the moments when you're inclined to think it's worth paying hundreds of dollars a night to stay here.

The lobby of the Ritz Hotel in Paris is small, as is the staircase, but both are elegant. As the revolving door glides to a stop behind you, and the concierge summons the porter for your bags, you know that for a couple of days, that lobby and that staircase will belong to you. César Ritz said he wanted his hotel to have 'all the refinements of living that a prince might hope to incorporate in his own town house'. And for as long as he or she is there, each guest should be royalty.

Now picture any so-called grand hotel built in the last 20 years. You can hardly sweep into the lobby from a bank of elevators. And even if there is a staircase, the lobby is as big as an air terminal, filled with people and suitcases just off the last tour bus. Your waiting friends can't even find you, let alone admire the awesomeness of your entrance. The modern hotel may have marble columns and frothing fountains, but it caters for the throng, not the individual. Your Regents, your Hyatts, your Renaissances, your Sheratons are rarely in Ritzonia. For that, you must return to the Ritz in Paris, the Danieli in Venice, the Beau-Rivage in Lausanne, and the Peninsula in Hong Kong. Their stories are illuminating.

Most people think the idea of the grand hotel originated in Switzerland, but actually the fad started in the United States. In the 1820s, American entrepreneurs speculated that rich travellers might like to stay in replicas of the palaces where European aristocrats lived, instead of the humble inns they were used to. The Tremont in Boston became the biggest and most luxurious hotel in the world when it opened in 1829. Clad in white granite, it had 170 rooms and a dining room seating 200, with such revolutionary features as an individual key for each bedroom, 'French cuisine', stables separated from the main building, eight baths with cold running water in the basement and eight toilets on the ground floor. Most amazing of all, each guest was given a free bar of soap.

British businessmen soon emulated the Americans, building elaborate accommodations in spa towns or near railway junctions. And in Venice, which had already been a tourist town for 300 years, a small but elite establishment began to grow in the 15th century Palazzo Dandolo near Piazza San Marco. The guesthouse, which was opened in 1822 by Giuseppe dal Niel, could claim to be the world's first embassy of Ritzonia, even before the founder of that state was born. From the 1830s it was the Venetian hangout for such luminaries as Charles Dickens, Richard Wagner, John Ruskin, Marcel Proust and Honoré de Balzac. The novelist George Sand and the poet Alfred de Musset held orgies in their room during a holiday there in 1833, and when de Musset fell sick, Sand had an affair with the doctor. In 1840, when he was able to buy more space in the building, Dal Niel christened the hotel after his nickname—Danieli.

The Danieli cast its spell on new arrivals from the moment they entered the lobby and saw the yellow marble staircase zig-zagging up one wall in front of them. These days, if you use that staircase instead of the tiny lift, you find yourself in a maze of corridors with inexplicable twists that suggest the place has been cobbled together over the past century from a variety of structures. Insist on a room in the original palace, and you'll end up in a tapestried chamber with a briarwood bed big enough to sleep four, and a tiny balcony overlooking the Grand Canal. You'll realise that Ritzonia is not just another country but another time.

In the 1850s, winter sports started to become fashionable with Europeans, and Switzerland ski-jumped into the grand hotel game. The Beau-Rivage Palace in Lausanne opened in 1861, with 150 bedrooms overlooking Lake Geneva, and kept expanding. It was soon able to offer its guests a pet cemetery, in case Mitzi or Brutus should pass away during the holiday. But human hygiene was less important, apparently. As the hotel was being built, the first manager, Alexandre Rufenacht, eliminated all the bathrooms from the architects' plan 'because they use up too much water'. Guests who wanted hot water could have it brought from the kitchen by maids, and for a full-scale bath, they could use a special 'bathing cabin' in a house adjacent to the hotel.

César Ritz took a different view of private ablutions. When he opened his own hotel on the Place Vendome, Paris, in 1898, he attached a bathroom to every bedroom. But it had been a long journey for him to reach that point, and he had seen his share of squalor. Born in 1850 and barely educated, Ritz was apprenticed by his father at the age of 15 to a hotel restaurant in the town of Brig. He was dismissed as incompetent after a few months, and made his way to Paris. He was working in a restaurant called Voisin's during the Franco-Prussian War of 1870, when a siege brought the city to the edge of starvation. Voisin's started to specialise in rats and mice, and Ritz later recalled that 'the finest ragout of rabbit I ever ate came from a skinny alley cat'. When an elephant died in the Paris zoo, Ritz persuaded the restaurant to buy it and offer the clients elephant's blood sausage and *tronc d'elephant sauce chasseur.*

Ritz began a habit of writing the whims of the richest customers in a little notebook, and soon his talent for providing personal attention brought him job offers from other restaurants and hotels. His passion for hygiene developed when he was managing the Victoria Hotel in San Remo, on the Italian Riviera, in 1875. Many of the guests were there to recover from tuberculosis, and Ritz concluded that germs could breed in the dust that accumulated on the heavy velvet drapes, on the wallpaper, and on top of wardrobes. He declared that when he designed his own hotel, all the fabrics would be washable, the walls would be painted, the cupboards would be built-ins, and every room would have a bathroom. His wife Marie-Louise later boasted that Ritz was 'one of the greatest civilising influences of his time as regards this point of sanitation and hygiene'.

At the age of 27, he became manager of the Grand Hotel Nationale in Lucerne, and turned it into the most fashionable resort in Europe. He enticed from Paris a chef named Auguste Escoffier and the two began a 25-year partnership which changed the way the world thought about eating and accommodation. Escoffier invented the *a la carte* menu, allowing guests a wide choice of dishes instead of what the hotelier felt like giving them. As Ritz and Escoffier moved from hotel to hotel across Europe during the 1880s, they were followed by what Ritz called 'my gilded caravan of nomads'— people such as Edward, the Prince of Wales, assorted European aristocrats and entertainers, and Wall Street royalty such as the Vanderbilts and the Morgans.

In 1889, Ritz and Escoffier were recruited by the British businessman Richard d'Oyly Carte to bring the crowds to the Savoy Hotel in London. When the Savoy opened, its first brochure made these dramatic promises: 'Electric light everywhere and at all times. No gas. Large and luxurious lifts working without interruption. Corridors heated day and night. 70 bathrooms'.

While the Savoy was being built, the contractor had queried the need for 70 bathrooms, and asked d'Oyly Carte if he was expecting his clients to be amphibious. Ritz's notions of cleanliness were still too radical for his time.

Ritz's approach to hospitality was radical too. He lobbied for a change in hotel licensing laws to allow him to keep serving dinner after 11 p.m. on weeknights and to open for dinner on Sundays. He was accused of destroying English family life by attracting men to eat away from their homes, and by allowing ladies to dine without their husbands.

Ritz spent the 1890s accumulating money and friends, and in 1896—while still working for the Savoy— he bought a mansion in the Place Vendome, Paris, and began reconstructing its interior. Some of his usual backers refused to join the project because they thought the space was too small to allow a profitable hotel, but Ritz replied that size was not necessarily the same as greatness. He filled the place with furniture modelled on what he had seen in Versailles Palace, and the most lavish artworks, crystal and linen. He installed the world's first indirect lighting, using wall sconces which shone onto the ceilings instead of onto the customers' faces. He had toilet seats specially moulded to be more comfortable than the standard of the day, and laid down a cellar of 180,000 wine bottles. The funding for most of this came from a brave wine dealer called Marnier la Postolle, who made an orange-flavoured brandy which Ritz had christened 'Grand Marnier' and served at the Savoy.

Early in 1898, Ritz and Escoffier left the Savoy under mysterious circumstances. Much later, it was revealed that they were found pilfering. They had done deals to receive percentages of what the Savoy paid to food suppliers, and skimmed funds from various other enterprises within the hotel. To avoid a public scandal, d'Oyly Carte let them pay back some of the money and say they were resigning because of arguments with the head housekeeper. D'Oyly Carte even managed to hold his tongue when the Prince of Wales declared he would no longer patronise the Savoy because 'where Ritz goes, I go'.

The mystery was soon overshadowed by the opening, in Paris on 1 June 1898, of the hotel that Ritz had been building for two years. Ritz called it 'the first modern hotel in Paris . . . hygienic, efficient and beautiful'. It was an immediate success, particularly when the Prince of Wales (soon to be Edward VII) moved his custom there from the Hotel Bristol.

Ritz could have rested on those laurels, but he went on to open a hotel called the Carlton in London (where Escoffier named a peach dessert and a toast speciality after an Australian soprano named Nellie Melba) and start planning projects in New York, Cairo and South Africa. But his perfectionism had turned into fanaticism. He would spend hours instructing the chambermaids how to make beds, and choosing just the right shade of pink for the lampshades to complement the complexions of female guests. In 1903, as he was contemplating how a Ritz hotel could be built in London, he suffered the first of several nervous breakdowns. His wife Marie-Louise took over the running of the Paris Ritz. She said later that César 'gradually sank out of life. A dark cloud seemed to envelop his mind. It lifted only at brief intervals during the 15 years that elapsed before death released him'. The family put him in a clinic at Kussnacht, near Lucerne, and he spent his final years making clay models of his dog, again and again and again.

But other hotels were benefiting from his influence. Back in Switzerland, the Beau-Rivage finally got around to adding bathrooms, and became Europe's principal centre for diplomatic travellers. The peace treaty which ended the Italo-Turkish war was signed there in 1912, amid much banqueting. In 1923, Turkey and the Allies signed the Treaty of Lausanne there, and in 1933 the Beau-Rivage housed the British delegation to the Reparations Conference between the great powers of Europe. (Even as recently as 1984, the hotel hosted a conference designed to bring peace in Lebanon, but the bracing Swiss air can only do so much.)

Along with the political heavies came the literary and theatrical stars. The Beau-Rivage visitors' book for the 40s and 50s contains frequent repetitions of Somerset Maugham, Noel Coward, Charles Chaplin, Maurice Chevalier, Gary Cooper and Ginger Rogers. The designer Coco Chanel, who had been as revolutionary for women's fashions as César Ritz was for accommodations, managed to drag herself away from the Paris Ritz, where she lived between 1930 and her death in 1971, to make annual journeys to Lausanne. Her companion, Michel Deon, wrote this diary entry in 1953: 'However enervating the atmosphere in Lausanne may have been, I rather liked the Beau-Rivage, under the management at the time of Mr Muller, a ponderously kind Swiss-German. His stupefaction knew no bounds at the sight of my sports car arriving first, roof down, Coco at my side wearing a veil of pink gauze like a motorist in the 1900s. Behind us followed the Cadillac driven by a liveried chauffeur, with two chambermaids on the plush grey seat, one gripping in her detergent-worn hands the famous jewel case as if she were taking the Blessed Sacrament to the condemned souls at the Beau-Rivage. Mr Muller greeted us on the threshold with the same question: "Did Mademoiselle come all right on her way?" '

Asia didn't really enter the grand hotel game until the 20th century, although Raffles in Singapore had been entertaining long-distance travellers since 1890. When the Peninsula Hotel opened in the unfashionable Kowloon district of Hong Kong in 1928, many locals thought it would be a white elephant. It proved to be a tiger. Its lobby, with enormous marble pillars topped with grimacing gargoyles, a surprisingly small grand staircase, and balconies carrying string quintets, came to be known as 'the meeting place of all Asia'. Within months of opening, the Peninsula was baptised into international stardom by the veteran hotel addict Charlie Chaplin (a regular at the Ritz and the Beau-Rivage).

The Peninsula was the venue for the formal surrender of British forces to Japanese forces on Christmas Day 1941, and the Governor of Hong Kong, Sir Mark Young, was imprisoned in room 336 until February 1942. It was renamed the Toa Hotel and became the headquarters of the new Japanese governor until September 1945, when Japanese and British officials met there to arrange the transfer of power again.

Over the same period, the Ritz in Paris was under German occupation. They took the side of the building facing the Place Vendome and consigned guests such as Coco Chanel to the back. But the staff got their revenge, keeping the Resistance informed of German activities by a code conveyed in the way foodstuffs were ordered. Ernest Hemingway, another collector of grand hotels, claimed to have personally liberated the Ritz in 1945 by driving up in a jeep with General David Bruce and cracking the first bottle of champagne in the bar now named after him. Hemingway supposedly said: 'When I dream of an afterlife in heaven, the action always takes place in the Paris Ritz'.

From the 1950s, The Ritz, under César's ageing son Charles, went into a genteel decline. It was bought from the Ritz family in 1979 for $30 million by an Egyptian businessman named Mohammed Al Fayed. He spent $130 million on a ten-year renovation program that included excavating deep under the Place Vendome to build a night club, a gymnasium and a swimming pool reminiscent of the most decadent Roman baths. The Ritz has revived its old motto: 'luxury, perfection and discretion'.

The Beau-Rivage is still a retreat for the royalty of the modern age. During the Montreux Jazz Festival each year, Woody Allen (also a regular at the Ritz) used to move in for a couple of weeks with several of his children—now he just brings one of Mia Farrow's adopted daughters. Diana Ross held a wedding and honeymoon there in the early 90s, joined by friends such as Stevie Wonder and Gregory Peck (also a regular at both the Ritz and the Peninsula).

The Beau-Rivage distinguishes itself from other hotels of my experience by quietly putting under your door at 6am a slip of paper on which the day's weather forecast is indicated by diagrams that include a sun, a cloud, an umbrella and a snowflake. I was also impressed with the way a jacket that I had left on the train bringing me to Lausanne appeared in my room within 24 hours of my asking the concierge if there was anything he could do to help.

The Peninsula, under a series of Swiss managers, has managed to combine lavish service (four staff to a room, while most grand hotels have two) with a big investment in new technology. Guests are still carried to and from the airport in Rolls-Royces. Tradition-minded customers still observe the protocol that British people and attached ladies take their tea on the right side of the lobby while other nationalities and ladies 'seeking dalliance' sit on the left (something of a dilemma if you're a romantic lady who is also British). Every room now has a fax machine (which prints out your phone messages); TV sets in bedroom and bathroom; a laser video player (and a library of discs); and a panel by the bed which controls the airconditioning, displays the indoor and outdoor temperature, turns on the 'Do Not Disturb' sign, summons room service, and opens and closes the curtains.

But remember where you are. The guest information booklet declares: 'The Peninsula would like to offer its guests a distinguished lifestyle. Therefore guests are requested not to wear shorts, singlets, flip flops or slippers in the hotel's public areas'.

The Peninsula has demonstrated its optimism about the communist takeover of Hong Kong in 1997 by adding two new towers with an extra 130 rooms, two helipads, a rooftop swimming pool and a nightclub designed to appeal to 'chuppies' (upwardly mobile young Chinese). Its management is convinced that communists, perhaps more than most of us, need the fantasy of Ritzonia.

19 · SICILY

At first sight, the word *penisola* might suggest an unusual sort of musical instrument, perhaps along the lines of a pipe organ. You see the word often in Sicily, and you may be reluctant to ask what it means. To save embarrassment, let me tell you *la penisola* is the Sicilian name for Italy. As far as the Sicilians are concerned, the long strip of land that includes such dumps as Milan, Florence and Rome is just a peninsula that connects Europe with Sicily.

On the wine list at the Villa Sant'Andrea, which is a pleasant hotel on the beach below Taormina, you will encounter a lot of terrific Sicilian whites such as Regaliali and Etna and reds such as Corvo and Faro and stickies such as Marsala and Malvasia. Then in a small space at the bottom of the page, under the heading 'Vini della Penisola', you'll find Chianti, Orvieto, Frascati and other stuff that only an eccentric would want to know about.

Sicilians believe their island is another country, and

this separatism doesn't disturb the Penisolans at all. To the extent that Sicily is different from Italy, the difference is mostly to the traveller's advantage. Sicily has a reputation for killing people, but they tend to be local residents or magistrates visiting from the penisola. For travellers, the island has an openness and an innocence that is rare in the rest of Europe and particularly on the penisola. Sicily seems not yet to be jaded by tourism.

Extraordinary historical sites are left open to be wandered over at will. If the locals were as criminal as their reputation, you'd think they would have sold off all the antiquities by now, but they seem surprised that anyone is interested. 'Well, yes,' they might say, 'I suppose that is a 3000-year-old temple on the hill there. Go and climb on it if you like. I'll be just sitting here picking my teeth.'

If modern Italy is over-civilised, then modern Sicily remains savage in a way that explains why the countryside around Florence became an obsession with the English a century ago. You get the feeling that the characters in *A Room With A View* experienced something like Sicily is now before the Tuscans realised how much they could charge for everything.

The downside is that you can't see Sicily quickly. My plan was to do a clockwise circuit of the island from Palermo to Taormina in four days, stopping at only the essential sites. I didn't know that you need to allow another three days for getting lost. Sicilians don't bother much with signposts, because they know where they're going and they haven't yet realised that strangers might want to find something in particular.

I flew into the airport at Palermo and hired a car, heading for the once grand hotel Villa Igiea, supposedly a half-hour drive. Getting into town was an ulcerous experience. The Sicilians like to drive five abreast on two-lane highways and don't recognise red lights. They will overtake you on either side at any time. Map reading is useless because most streets are unmarked—the signs have either fallen off or faded to illegibility. Even if you speak Italian it's not much use asking the way, because these people speak Sicilian, and anyway, many citizens of Palermo seem to suffer from speech impediments. What they are most likely to tell you is *sempre dritto*, which means 'straight ahead', but since the main roads of Palermo keep changing into one-way streets coming the other way, this is not helpful.

Reaching the Villa Igiea took two hours, so that at 3 p.m. they regretted that the only lunch they could make for me was a plate of sliced tomatoes, basil leaves and mozzarella cheese drizzled with olive oil. It was sensational: the tomatoes plump and flavourful, the cheese made from buffalo milk, the olive oil dense and green. It also turned out to be one of the best meals I had in Sicily.

The disappointment of Sicily is the food. For all the legends about a complex cuisine blended from Sicily's various invaders—the Greeks, the Arabs, the Normans, the Spanish and the Penisolans—the reality is that every restaurant specialises in grilled swordfish and *pasta con le sarde*, which is thick spaghetti with sardines, fennel, onions, raisins and almonds. It's fine the first time, but by the fifth day, you're desperate for something new.

Fortunately I found a novelty in Catania, an industrial town on the east coast that is worth visiting only for a restaurant called La Siciliana. A dish called *rippidu nivicatu*, which I ordered on the principle that the words looked odd, turned out to be a mound of black risotto made with squid ink, topped with white ricotta cheese and a splash of spicy tomato puree. An hour later I realised that it was a visual pun when I drove past Mount

Etna, a volcano with its base covered with black ash, its top covered with snow and the occasional spurt of molten lava.

But Sicily has compensations for the apparent loss of its food heritage. It is, for example, very good at mysterious ruins. At Segesta, about two hours' drive southwest of Palermo, a massive limestone temple that almost leaves the Parthenon in the shade, stands on a hill in the middle of nowhere. Scholars keep speculating about what god the temple was built for, and why it was left unfinished. My favourite theory is that it was built as a public relations exercise. Around 450 BC, the inhabitants of the area then called Egesta (the later addition of the 's' may be something to do with those speech impediments I mentioned earlier) were fighting a territorial war with their neighbours in the coastal town of Selinus. They asked Athens to join them in a mutual defence pact, and started building the temple (using a Greek architect) to show the Athenians they were *their* sort of people. In 416 BC, the Athenians, duly impressed, sent troops to help the Egestans clobber Selinus, but they were ignominiously defeated (because the Selinusians had made their own defence pact with Syracuse, on the other side of Sicily). The Egestans, not wanting to be associated with a bunch of losers, downed tools and just left the 36 Doric columns standing there to mystify future generations. Then they made an alliance with the Carthaginians, who moved in and smashed Selinus. Centuries later, Egesta was destroyed by Muslim invaders, and all that is left of the devious civilisation on the hill is their expensive PR exercise and a modest amphitheatre.

The people of Selinus (now called Selinunte) were enthusiastic temple builders too. Drive from Segesta to the coastline half an hour away and you can clamber on the ruins of three temples that are at least 200 years older than the PR exercise, though not as well preserved. They seem to be genuine attempts to honour such celebrities as Apollo and Hercules. Amongst them you'll find souvenir sellers offering Greek relics of the 5th century BC (fresh from the factory), and across the road you'll see modern Selinuntians sunbaking on polluted Marinella beach.

The best ruins are near the town of Agrigento. If you stay in a hotel called the Villa Politi, you can see them from your balcony and reach them simply by walking through the hotel's olive grove and hopping over a stone fence. There's a row of nine temples built around 450 BC, and a massive fallen statue (seven metres long) that looks like a sunbaking giant. The Temple of Olympian Zeus is the biggest in the world (113 metres long by 54 metres wide), but most of it has collapsed. The golden Temple of Concord is the best preserved in Sicily (because it was used as a Christian church till the 18th century) and at sunset on Saturdays it's the favourite spot in Agrigento for the taking of wedding photos.

If you're all templed out by now, you can leap back to the 20th century and visit the nearby birthplace of the Nobel prize winner Luigi Pirandello, who wrote the play *Six Characters in Search of an Author*. He was born in a village called Caos, which is appropriate.

The island also does a nice line in pretty towns with no visible populations. The quaintest is Erice, which should be in France instead of on a clifftop on the west coast of Sicily. Narrow cobbled streets apparently used only by cats lead up to a spectacular castle built by the Normans in the 14th century out of stones pinched from a Greek temple on the same spot. The most creepy town is Corleone, but no doubt I was letting my imagination run away with me because Salvatore Riina, the 'boss of bosses' accused of ordering more than 100 murders, lived there for 20 years till his arrest in 1993. No wonder Mario Puzo named his Godfather after it.

Near another Norman town, Piazza Armerina, archaeologists in the 1950s uncovered a Roman villa from the 3rd century AD with the most beautiful mosaic floors in the world. You can walk over bridges of scaffolding and look down at 40 scenes of recreations enjoyed 1600 years ago. There are chariot races, girls in bikinis playing volleyball, children chasing rabbits and ducks, adults hunting lions and tigers which are now extinct, cherubs riding sea serpents, and lots and lots of feasting.

After the silence of those places, Taormina comes as a shock. A 20-minute drive up a series of hairpin bends is followed by a half-hour search for a parking spot, because Taormina is buried under tourists, most of whom seem to be German. Cars are banned from the main street, Corso Umberto, but that doesn't prevent you from being knocked over by backpacks. There are sensational views, if you can see them between the bodies. D. H. Lawrence lived in a villa on Via Fontana Vecchia in the early 1920s, but then, it's hard to find a town in Europe where D. H. Lawrence didn't live. He is certainly not a reason to linger in Taormina.

Syracuse, by contrast, is an essential stop, and not only because it was the home of Archimedes, one of the greatest icons of physics and geometry. Syracuse is Sicily's liveliest town, a title it has held since 500 BC, when it became the Manhattan of the Mediterranean.

Archimedes discovered the principle of displacement of water there in 230 BC, leaping from his bath and running down the street shouting Eureka ('I have it'). The locals tolerated his eccentricities because he was good at making weapons of mass destruction to stop the Romans from invading. He built slingshots that smashed the Romans' ladders with 200-kilogram lead weights, and cranes that pulled the Roman ships out of the water. He supposedly figured out a system of mirrors and lenses that focused the sun's rays and set fire to sails. But the Penisolans managed to sneak into Syracuse anyway, by which time Archimedes was back at his desk engaging in his first love—mathematics. He was so busy working out the value of pi that he didn't realise a Roman had entered his room until the soldier ran him through with a sword.

There's a statue of Archimedes at Syracuse's Porta Licea, with a big white beard and a toga falling off his hips. He is looking out to sea with a giant lens on a corkscrew in his right hand. There's also a good little restaurant called Archimede on the island of Ortygia (connected to Syracuse by several bridges), offering a bigger choice of seafood than the usual swordfish.

But these tributes hardly do the genius justice. If the Syracusans had any commercial sense, they'd set up The Archimedes Experience, charging visitors to test their weight in a replica of the great man's bath, or set fire to model ships, or build weapons out of weights and pulleys, or watch a re-enactment of the disembowelling. But that's the sort of thing entrepreneurs would do on the Penisola. In Sicily, they might get around to it in 100 years.

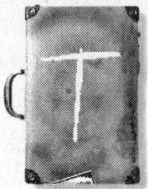

20 · TOLEDO, SPAIN

The main hall of the Transito synagogue in Toledo is empty of furniture and statuary. Its story can only be read in its intricately decorated walls, where, through traceries of wood and alabaster, you can make out a mingling of symbols—Christian castles and coats of arms, Muslim crescents, and Jewish candlesticks under Hebrew slogans.

To a modern mind, such a blending of the world's stubbornest and most mutually antagonistic faiths is impossible. But it happened for a short golden age back in the 14th and 15th centuries, when the building that was later called El Transito became the intellectual powerhouse of the world. Scholars from the Islamic culture, the Jewish culture and the Christian culture journeyed to Toledo, then the capital of Spain, to share their knowledge. They worked in the synagogue with teams of translators provided by the Spanish royal family. They exchanged ideas on science, music, medicine, philosophy and alchemy, collaborating to advance the wisdom of the entire human race. Moorish artisans fashioned the wall carvings and mouldings to symbolise the collaboration.

Standing under the high ceiling of El Transito, you can picture these bearded men at their benches, poring over manuscripts amid a babble of voices. In a book called *The Jews of Spain*, Jane S. Gerber described the scene: 'Being multilingual, Jews could easily render the Arabic text into a Castilian or Catalan version that a Christian scholar would translate into Latin. This project was truly cooperative in practice as well as spirit, for scholars worked by reading aloud to each other. Scientists would create as they translated, in the process forming new syntheses of knowledge. Scholars were swarming into the city from other parts of Europe, making Toledo the continent's entryway for the knowledge that had come from the east in mathematics, philosophy, medicine, botany and practical geometry'.

At the time, the Jewish name for Spain was Sepharad, an ancient Biblical term for a kind of earthly paradise. Toledo was Sepharad's capital. It was how the Jews imagined Jerusalem had been in ancient times, and would be again one day.

For 1000 years the Jews of Spain lived in what they considered a magical period of scholarship, creativity and collaboration with other religions. From the collapse of the Roman Empire in the 4th century, they had survived invasions by the Visigoths, a takeover in the 8th century by a North African Muslim people called the Moors (who made the Jews their negotiators with the Christian community) and the 'reconquest' by Christian nobility in 1085. Initially the Christian rulers were delighted by the opportunity to learn from the Moors and the Jews in Toledo. The Transito synagogue was built in 1357 to be a home for the flourishing information exchange. But by the 15th century, fundamentalism was on the rise. In 1479 the Inquisition was set up to encourage Jews and Muslims to convert to Christianity and to ensure that the *conversos* were not secretly engaging in Jewish rituals. Citizens were encouraged to spy on their neighbours and note any 'unChristian behaviour'—which even included making a stew, since the use of a slow cooking method might mean you were preparing for the Sabbath (when orthodox Jews can do no work). This was the origin of the modern Spanish obsession with pork sausages—if you had strings of chorizo hanging in your kitchen, you showed the Inquisition's spies you were non-kosher.

The terminal year for Sepharad was 1492, when King Ferdinand and Queen Isabella, often portrayed as among history's great visionaries and risk-takers, made two decisions that transformed the world. Christopher Columbus referred to both decisions in his journal: 'After the Spanish monarchs had expelled all the Jews from their kingdoms and lands in January, in that same month they commissioned me to undertake the voyage to India with a properly equipped fleet'.

The immediate cause of the expulsion of the Jews was the conquest of Granada, the last city under Moorish control (an expedition largely financed with borrowings from Jewish courtiers). Ferdinand and Isabella decided Spain should be a purely Christian nation. They issued the Decree of Expulsion, under which 300,000 Jews were given the choice of converting to Christianity or leaving the country within four months. The decree proclaimed: 'Since it is clearly demonstrated that they always try by all means at their disposal to destroy and draw away the Christian believers from our Holy Catholic faith, to separate them from it, to bring them near to their faith . . .

by initiating Christians into their rituals and religious customs, by organising assemblies in which they read to them and teach them and their children ... giving them from their houses the unleavened bread and ritually slaughtered meat ... we have agreed to order the expulsion of all Jews and Jewesses in our kingdom. And if they are found living in our kingdoms and domains they should be put to death'.

The Muslims faced the same choice soon afterwards. The Inquisition rapidly disposed of those who tried to continue Toledo's great experiment. The synagogue where the exchange of ideas had taken place was turned into a Christian church called El Transito. The Spanish capital was moved to Madrid.

The Inquisition continued to seek out and punish Jewish sympathisers for another 300 years. If you stand these days in the elegant little Plaza Mayor in central Madrid, you can picture how it could work as an open-air courtroom, where suspected anti-Catholics were tried and punished. Bleachers were set up on the left and right so the populace could get a good view of the interrogations taking place in the middle. Special guests in the audience, such as visiting nobility, were given the honour of lighting the pyre under the convicted prisoners. These entertainments were called *autos da fe* (a Portuguese term meaning 'act of faith'). During the slow bits the crowds could admire the paintings on the facades of the buildings.

When the Decree of Expulsion was issued, about 100,000 Sephardic Jews decided to convert to Christianity. The rest went into exile, making a trail which today we can follow to the Middle East, southern France, Venice, Rome, Amsterdam and ultimately across the Atlantic to the New World. Many went initially to Portugal, where, for a huge fee, King John granted an eight-month entry permit. Some began a land trek which took them to the Netherlands, where religious intolerance was giving way to an appreciation of skills in literacy and trade. They were soon among the first to develop the new Dutch colonies in America.

Many became boat people around the Mediterranean, finding temporary refuge (and public resentment) in such cities as Marseilles and Naples, where a local historian described them leaving their boats on 24 August 1492: 'One might have taken them for spectres, so emaciated were they, and with eyes so sunken—they differed in nothing from the dead, except in the power of motion, which indeed they scarcely retained'.

Longer term, thousands of Sephardic Jews ended up in Venice, which set up a Jewish suburb near some foundries that used to make cannons. The area was called the ghetto (from the word *ghettare*, 'to cast in iron'). These days it is behind the railway station (near S. Marcuola vaporetto stop on the Grand Canal). As the foundries closed and space became available, Venice's Jewish population spread to an adjoining island called the Ghetto Nuovo, where a nightly curfew was enforced by locked and guarded gates. As the population kept growing in the late 16th century, they built upwards, and produced Europe's first high-rise apartment blocks—seven-storey buildings still inhabited today. The Jews of Venice weren't persecuted—they were simply ripped off. The rents they had to pay to live in the ghetto grew so exorbitant that in 1735 the colony inside the gates went bankrupt. In 1797 the gates were pulled down by the French, and the children of Sepharad were finally allowed to live where they pleased.

When the Jews and Muslims left it, Toledo fell into

rapid decline. Today it is a beautiful shell that survives on tourism, looking a lot like Venice without the canals. Most of its visitors don't go near the Juderia, the Jewish quarter, unless they are seeking the former home of the painter El Greco. Mostly they come on day trips from Madrid to see the Cathedral and the Alcazar and to eat stuffed partridge, which is the town's speciality (my *perdiz estofada a la toledana*, served in a place called Asador Adolfo, was overcooked but that's how the Spanish like it).

The towering Alcazar was once a Moorish fortress but is now a place of pilgrimage for the fascists of the world, because in 1936 a group of Franco supporters locked themselves in there and held out against Republican troops for two months. The interior is dotted with plaques complimenting the Francoists on their bravery, donated by such groups as the Chilean Army, the Argentinian Army and the 'Croatian Nazis in Exile'. Some of those visitors may have been responsible for the swastika I saw spraypainted on the wall of a house in the Juderia.

The small Jewish community in Spain has plans to turn the remains of Transito synagogue into a museum of the holocaust. I hope they don't. There are already holocaust museums elsewhere in the world, reminding us of the depths to which human beings can sink. But by its emptiness, the synagogue in Toledo says much more about the heights that human beings can reach. We got there, just briefly, 600 years ago. Perhaps we can again.

21 · UNION SQUARE, NEW YORK

First timers in Manhattan often head for Times Square, thinking it is the heart of the city. They are disappointed to find a clump of clogged arteries, surrounded by ugly office blocks and porno cinemas. If a heart symbolises life, generosity, passion and humanity, then the heart of Manhattan is Union Square. Sometimes in its history Union Square has beaten almost too fast and too loudly for the city to bear—like the weekend in 1927 when police mounted machine-guns on the roofs of the surrounding buildings in case a workers' meeting in the square got out of hand.

The workers were protesting about the execution of two labour organisers named Nicola Sacco and Bartolomeo Vanzetti, who had been sentenced to death for murder despite purely circumstantial evidence and a confession by another man. The police didn't need their machine-guns—horses and batons were enough to subdue the crowd on that day, if not in the long term. Through the 20s and 30s, Union Square became the rallying point for left-wing causes and soapbox orators of all kinds. The communists, the anarchists, *The Daily Worker* newspaper and many trade unions set up their headquarters in the blocks around it. In 1930 as the Depression worsened, 35,000 unemployed people met in Union Square, clashed violently with the police, and marched to City Hall demanding jobs. For a time, the radicals of New York thought Union Square was going to be the birthplace of America's socialist revolution.

Flourishing unionism in the heart of Manhattan, a few blocks up the road from Wall Street, the bastion of capitalism? That's just one of the many paradoxes that Union Square has thrown up in its 160-year zig-zag between squalor and splendour. The latest is apparent on any Saturday morning, when the farmers of New York State and Pennsylvania drive into Manhattan and set up The Green Market, a semi-circle of stalls displaying fresh fruit, vegetables, sausages, organic wines, flowers and home-baked pies, as well as books, furnishings and bits of junk that have become surplus to needs at the farmhouse. Country folk coming to town to sell their produce is one of the most ancient rituals of the human race, but to see it still happening at the end of the 20th century in the heart of the most jaded urban concentration on earth is both surprising and reassuring.

The Union Square Green Market is the closest most Manhattanites ever get to fresh food, so it gets about 70,000 customers every Saturday. The throng displays the human contrasts on which America thrives—polo-shirted yuppies with mobile phones bulging from their chinos, closely questioning bearded Amish folk and ponytailed hippies in leather aprons about the best ways to cook pumpkin pie. I copied down these hand-lettered signs as I strolled round the market:

Radishes. Asparagus. HERBS spearmint, cilantrillo, sweet marjoram, basil flowers.
Martin's handmade pretzels.
All apples and cider. Home baked fruit tarts.
Fresh milk from no hormone cows. Cheeses.
Keith's farm organic produce—mizuna, tetsoi, flowering chives.
All CDs, Cassettes, LPs, $5.
Bluefish pate. Pheasant. Wild turkey. Rabbits.
Fiddleheads! Young ferns picked just as they emerge from the ground. $2 a pint.
Balloon twister.
Hawthorne Valley Farm organic yoghurt.
Maple syrup candy.
The sweetest lettuce in the world grown on the black rich soil of Goshen, NY.
Homemade organic granola. Nut bread, Raisin scones.

As part of their celebration of peace, love and fruitfulness, the people who run the Green Market wrap coloured robes around the statue of Gandhi which stands at one corner of the square and place baskets of fresh vegetables in front of him.

Across the road, at 33 Union Square, there's another 20th century icon. This thin overdecorated terrace house was the headquarters of the artist Andy Warhol during the 1960s. He called it The Factory, and made such movies as *Blow Job, Flesh* and *Sleep* there. In 1968 Valerie Solanis, a member of a group called SCUM (Society for Cutting Up Men) strode into The Factory and started firing a pistol at Warhol because he had rejected her film script and because he symbolised male oppression of women.

At the time, Union Square was going through one of its seedy phases so Warhol's rent was cheap. Nobody went into the grassy middle of the square unless they wanted to buy drugs or find a bench to sleep on for the night. It was difficult back then to see how Union Square could have been Manhattan's most fashionable district through most of the 19th century. In the 1840s it was where a group of sporting gents known as the Knicker-bocker Club first codified the rules of a game called base-ball. In the 1870s it was at one end of 'Ladies' Mile', a row of expensive department stores that sprawled along Broadway from 23rd Street to 17th Street (their fabulous facades are still visible, covered with soot and posters). In the 1880s the square was surrounded by playhouses, bars, nightclubs, grand hotels, music halls and brothels. In 1902, what was then the world's tallest skyscraper was erected just up the road—the Flatiron Building on the corner of Broadway and 23rd Street. Its triangular shape sets up skirt-lifting gusts of wind and it became a popular spot for men to catch glimpses of ladies' calves. The police instruction for the men to move along—'23 skidoo'—became a cool catchphrase of the 1920s.

There are many theories about how Union Square got its name, nearly all of them wrong. It had nothing to do with the labour activism of the 1920s. It had nothing to do with support for the Union cause in the American Civil War (which is how Union Square in San Francisco was named). Nor was it because of all the bizarre human unions that took place in the area, though the circus entrepreneur Phineas T. Barnum liked his customers to think so. Barnum presided over the uniting of General

Tom Thumb and the equally diminutive Lavinia Warren, who were the top attractions in Barnum's freak show. Their wedding in the local Grace Church, on the corner of Broadway and 10th Street, was the social highlight of 1863, attended by 5000 guests including four state governors, 13 army generals and countless moguls and millionaires.

And Union Square did not get its name because so many subway lines intersect beneath it, although it is certainly the best place in the city to attempt to understand the New York subway system. Descend into the smelly caverns beneath the square and you will find signs directing you to a grey line called L, orange lines called B, D, F and Q, green lines called 4, 5 and 6, and yellow lines called N and R. But how are you supposed to know if they go where you want? There's little point in asking directions, except as an exercise in hearing New Yorkers talk, because everybody has a different language for the routes. Old timers use names like the BMT (Brooklyn Manhattan Transfer) and the IRT (Interborough Rapid Transit). Younger types use numbers, colours or letters of the alphabet, depending on which attempt to simplify the system has won their allegiance. And even if they can describe the destinations of the trains, they can never quite explain which ones stop everywhere and which ones stop only occasionally. The problem is that New York started with several competing privately owned systems, which got amalgamated under a single under-funded government agency that has recently done a good job of cleaning up the carriages but still can't produce a map that makes sense. Best to come back upstairs and sit under a tree.

In fact, Union Square got its name for the most mundane reason. It was a park that was built at the union of two thoroughfares that were ploughed through Manhattan in 1830—Bloomingdale Road and Bowery Road, which later changed their names to Broadway and Park Avenue. If you'd got off the boat at the bottom of the island, Union Square was a pleasant resting place on your way to the top.

Having spent most of the 20th century in the doldrums, Union Square is just now entering glory days again, as symbolised by the presence on 16th Street of the Union Square Cafe, one of Manhattan's most exciting restaurants. I first heard of it via a rumour that it was the only place in America that served the world's greatest white wine by the glass. The experience inspired me to make a pilgrimage to the source of that wine, which I'll explain four chapters from now.

The Union Square Cafe is stimulating in many other ways. Its food is lively and diverse—somewhere between Italy and the American Deep South if you need a national origin, offering the likes of black bean soup ('with a dash of Australian sherry', says the menu), chicken liver risotto, calamari with anchovy dip, lamb cutlets on cous cous, baked chicken with polenta, and peach cobbler. The waiters, unlike many in Manhattan, are cheerful, helpful and unobtrusive. The barman is a human encyclopedia on the history and philosophy of wines. But don't offer to buy him a drink, because he'll politely decline on the grounds that he is 'a recovering alcoholic—these days I do it all by smell and memory'. And by now you're no longer surprised. Such paradoxes are standard in Union Square.

22 · VALLEY OF THE
KINGS, EGYPT

As we stepped out of the tomb of Tutankhamun, my daughter and I were so deep in conversation about death that we were almost skittled by a green delivery van turning out of High West Street into Allington Road. My daughter, just turned three, was fascinated by the black shrivelled corpse of the boy king. 'When will he wake up?' she asked. 'He won't wake up,' I said. 'He died a long time ago.' 'Why did he die?' she said. 'Because he fell out of his chariot and hit his head,' said I, discarding as too complicated the alternative theory (that Tut was murdered). 'He wasn't wearing his helmet!' she said, recalling an earlier discussion about how T. E. Lawrence (of Arabia) fell off his motorbike. 'That's right,' said I, hoping this would settle the matter. 'But when will he wake up?' she asked again. The issue of death is not to be dismissed so easily. I decided to go for diversion. 'He won't wake up,' I said, 'because that is just a statue. It's not a real person.' The narrowness of the footpath and the consequent need to jump back to avoid the van saved me from further prevarication.

Technically, the unwrapped mummy at The Tutankhamun Exhibition in the main street of Dorchester is not a statue. It is a human skeleton (formerly used by anatomy students), with the face bones restructured to look like the 19-year-old pharaoh and covered with animal skin which has been treated to look mummified. If you compare it with photos of the real Tut, you find it's not a bad imitation, and indeed, The Tutankhamun Exhibition is good entertainment for those whose interest in Tut is greater than their knowledge. You watch, for example, a re-enactment by waxwork figures of the lifting of the lid of Tut's massive sarcophagus by the archaeologist Howard Carter. You smell the incense that was almost certainly burning as the boy king was buried with his treasures. You see a substantial sampling of what Carter described in his first report as 'strange animals, statues and gold, everywhere the glint of gold'. You hear a dramatic narration by a voice I recognised as the one which delivered an equally momentous commentary during the sound and light show at the Temple of Karnak in Egypt.

Of course, nothing in The Tutankhamun Exhibition is more than ten years old, so the issue of authenticity may rear its head. The Dorchester presentation certainly offers a lot more than you could ever experience at Tut's real tomb in the Valley of the Kings. But it can never give the thrill of standing on the very spot where, on 26 November 1922, Howard Carter peeped through the hole he'd made in the door of a man-made cave on the west bank of the Nile and told his patron, Lord Carnarvon, that he could see 'wonderful things', starting an outbreak of mummy-mania from which the western world has not yet recovered. The fact that every year The Tutankhamun Exhibition at Dorchester gets 165,000 visitors—ten times the population of the town—is one tiny manifestation of the mania. Dorchester has no connection with Tutankhamun or Egypt or Howard Carter. A local entrepreneur simply decided in 1987 he could make a buck by exploiting the public obsession with the boy in the golden mask. And he was right.

Tutankhamun is in this book because he ranks with the likes of Sigmund Freud, Frank Lloyd Wright and Vincent van Gogh as a shaper of 20th century imagery. From the moment in 1922 when the British press announced Carter's discovery, the wonderful things in Tut's tomb inspired revolutions in fashion, design, architecture, movies, dance, advertising and literature. When Tut went on tour, millions shuffled through museums all over the world to examine his golden death mask and buy replicas of it in plaster, plastic and brass. In the words of the 1978 hit song by Steve Martin:

> Now if I'd known they'd line up just to see 'im,
> I'da taken all my money and bought me a museum.
> King Tut—buried with his donkey.
> King Tut—how'd you get so funky?
> Living by the Nile, ladies loved his style.
> He gave his life for tourism.

The boy king is the only Egyptian pharaoh to have achieved immortality, by an accident of history that left his tomb undisturbed until a century when mass-marketing could embed him in the collective consciousness.

In his own time (3200 years ago) Tutankhamun was

small potatoes, a teenager who sat on Egypt's throne for ten years as the puppet of priests and warriors. In the cosmic scheme of things, his father was far more significant. Tut's father, the pharaoh who called himself Akhenaten, was the first known proponent of perhaps the biggest idea the human race has ever thought—that only one god is running the universe, rather than many gods. At the time, Akhenaten's theory caused outrage, particularly among the priests who represented the 30 or so deities which the Egyptians were then worshipping. But the pharaoh didn't listen to his advisers, and used his army to suppress the old religion. He named his new god Aten (symbolised by a sun disc). He called himself 'he who benefits Aten', and his son 'living image of Aten' (Tutankhaten). For 17 years Egypt was in upheaval.

When Akhenaten's son became pharaoh at the age of nine, the priests fought back. The boy's name was changed to 'living image of Amun' (the sun god in the old religion). Tutankhamun did his best to obliterate all trace of his father's lone gunman scenario. But in the three millennia since then, the idea of god with a capital G has proved fairly influential.

Sigmund Freud spent his last four years working on a book called *Moses and Monotheism*, which argued that Akhenaten's theory was the inspiration for the Judeo-Christian belief system. Freud reckoned Moses was an Egyptian who merged Akhenaten's worship of Aten with the Midianites' worship of a volcano god called Yahweh and successfully sold the package to the Hebrews. When you look at the Great Hymn of the Aten, supposedly written by Akhenaten (and inscribed on the tomb wall of one of his favourite courtiers) you can't help noticing similarities to the language of the old testament:

How many are your deeds, though hidden from sight. O sole God beside whom there is none. You made the earth as you wished, you alone. All peoples, herds, and flocks. All upon earth that walk on legs. All on high that fly on wings . . .

This may seem like standard stuff to a modern reader, but nobody on the planet had heard anything like it before 1340 BC.

So Akhenaten was a pretty heavy hitter, and if you combine his religious influence with his son's impact on 20th century popular culture, you get a powerful reason to visit the old Egyptian city of Thebes, which included the places now called Karnak, Luxor and the Valley of the Kings. What follows is my suggestion on how to go about it.

To get there, you must take the 11-hour train journey from Cairo. You could fly directly into Luxor, but then you'd miss the experience of gliding back through time as the train leaves the slums of outer Cairo and begins to pass mud huts, white-robed farmers leading donkey carts, and water buffaloes neck deep in the Nile. At Luxor station you must take a *caleche* (a horse drawn carriage) rather than a taxi to your hotel. The caleche is not tourist kitsch but a practical way to travel over the mostly dirt roads of Luxor. You're supposed to bargain with the driver, and you should be able to get the fare down to about three Egyptian pounds from his initial bid of ten. I'm hopeless at that sort of thing and ended up agreeing to a package deal of 20 pounds, which covered being taken to my hotel and picked up half an hour later to be driven to Karnak temple and back. But the caleche driver, Hassanas, did let me sit up front with him and jiggle the reins.

The most interesting place to stay in Luxor is the

Old Winter Palace, across the road from the river bank. This is not because it is a good hotel. If I call it a model of faded grandeur, I'm putting the emphasis on faded. But it was where Lord Carnarvon stayed in 1922 while he and Carter were opening Tut's tomb. You can drink in the bar where the archaeologists celebrated their discovery. You can visit the suite where Carnarvon lay dying in 1923 from an infected mosquito bite, and thereby fed rumours that a 'mummy's curse' would fall on all who entered the tomb.

On your first morning, you could ease yourself into the Thebes experience by visiting Luxor temple, which is an easy walk from the Old Winter Palace and small enough not to be intimidating. Tutankhamun's grandfather, Amenophis III, started building the temple around 1380 BC in honour of the sun god Amun-Ra, but Akhenaten stopped the work because he didn't believe in Amun-Ra. The project was resumed in Tutankhamun's time, and you can see in the section called the Colonnade of Amenophis III some wall carvings that show Tut and his priests celebrating the revival of polytheism. Tut is on a boat with Amun-Ra, Ra's wife Mut (the vulture goddess) and their son Khonsu, the moon god. They seem glad to be back.

Inside a room called the Hypostyle Hall there's a bizarre bit of graffiti. Sometime in the 1880s the French poet Arthur Rimbaud scratched his name on the wall in large letters. But his writing is higher than any human arm could reach. Rimbaud must have been Rambo to have leapt up and clung long enough to carve his name. The explanation is that in Rimbaud's day, before the excavators got busy, the room was full of rubble, which meant that the 'floor' of the Hypostyle Hall was actually halfway up the wall.

You think Luxor Temple was impressive? It's a doll's house compared to Karnak. Now it's time to ride your caleche three kilometres northwards along the Nile and confront a construction project that lasted 1500 years and produced the world's biggest religious enclosure. Karnak dwarfs the pyramids. It could swallow Notre Dame Cathedral thirteen times. At one point (around 1250 BC), there were 81,000 slaves working inside it, building and maintaining the sandstone temples, lakes, columns, sphinxes, statues, pylons and labyrinths through which only priests and pharaohs were permitted to walk.

You must make two visits to Karnak—one by day to try to grasp the scale of it, and one by night to experience the *son et lumiere* show. The night spectacle is alternately funny and overwhelming. As you're shepherded around by torch-wielding guides, spotlights suddenly hit key elements of the statues and wallcarvings while a portentous voice, backed by a moaning choir, booms from hidden loudspeakers with such useful remarks as: 'The father is like unto an aged shepherd. His left hand fondles a wild ram walking with him. He is the god of the first day. It is he who is called Amun'.

Karnak is complicated because every pharaoh between 2000 BC and 400 BC made extensions and renovations, each trying to outdo his or her ancestors in permanent demonstrations of devotion. When Akhenaten inherited it, he made it the symbol of the new monotheism he was imposing on Egypt, partly as a political move to break the power of the priesthood. But the priests got their revenge. After Akhenaten died, the temples he built at Karnak were demolished and replaced by tributes to the gods he had suppressed. Akhenaten's name was systematically chipped off columns and walls, 28 gigantic statues of him were pulled off their pedestals, and images of his wife Nefertiti were defaced (although enough survived to make her image almost as influential on 'the Nile style' of the 20th century as the image of Tutankhamun). In historical records kept by the priests, Akhenaten was referred to as 'the damned one'. The lesson is: don't mess with the bureaucracy. The only visible remnants of Egypt's biggest troublemaker are the second, ninth and tenth pylons in the Great Court at Karnak. They are made of blocks taken from Akhenaten's vanished monuments to Aten.

And now you are ready for your final journey out of Luxor, to the place described by Howard Carter as 'remote from every sound of life ... Of all Egypt's wonders, there is none, I suppose, that makes more instant appeal to the imagination'. He was talking about the necropolis of Thebes, the Valley of the Kings, the place where 20 generations of pharaohs hid their wealth inside solid rock after they realised that the pyramids built by their ancestors were blatant invitations to tomb-robbers.

You should get up very early. The valley opens at 6am, because those who run it know that, by 1pm, the heat is unbearable, even for mad dogs and Englishmen. For this journey you'll need a taxi with a motor—taking a caleche would be too cruel to the horse—and you'll find lots of them waiting outside your hotel. Ask them to quote a half-day rate for driving you round the west bank, and bargain it down to half whatever they quote. You'll drive onto the car ferry across the Nile, queue for tickets to the tombs, and be approached by a million touts offering to sell you genuine 3000-year-old mummified ibises in clay pots. Then you'll drive over a hill and enter a vast barren landscape of rocks, pebbles and German backpackers. Sunglasses and a water bottle are vital.

I won't detain you with a rundown of the wonders in the valley, except to remark that number 17 is the most elaborate of the 60 visitable tombs cut into the limestone. It belonged to Seti I who took over Egypt 46 years after Tutankhamun died. Tut's tomb is numbered 62. Its four chambers are puzzlingly small after all you've heard about them, and you can't believe they once held more than 1700 wonderful things which now fill 12 galleries in the Museum of Egyptian Antiquities in Cairo.

What's left is the yellow quartzite sarcophagus from which Carter lifted the lid in 1922, using a block-and-tackle. These days the bottom half of the sarcophagus is covered with a glass slab to display one of the golden coffins (shaped to look like the pharaoh) which originally surrounded the body. Tutankhamun's blackened corpse is still inside that coffin. Although he was taken out several times for autopsies (which never could establish the cause of death), he is the only pharaoh who has been allowed to stay in the Valley of the Kings.

One wall of the burial chamber is decorated with blue baboons, who appear to be squatting on their own testicles. They wear expressions of grim resignation. Another wall shows the young pharaoh being greeted by Hathor, goddess of the west, who is placing a cross in his mouth to give him eternal life.

But what of Akhenaten? What's left of him? If you want to look on the revolutionary who failed to transform Egypt but who ended up transforming the world, you can try gallery three in Cairo's Museum of Egyptian Antiquities. It contains four statues which once straddled Akhenaten's temple at Karnak. The pharaoh's long thin face suggests that the ideal person to play him in a movie version of *Moses and Monotheism* would be Jerry Seinfeld.

The location of Akhenaten's body remains a mystery.

He had himself buried in a part of Egypt now called Armana, about halfway between Cairo and Luxor, where he was attempting to set up a new capital city. He called his new city Akhetaten (horizon of the Aten). As soon as Tutankhamun came to power, the royal court moved back to Thebes, and Tut later moved his father's body to somewhere in the Valley of the Kings.

If you have time after visiting Tut, try to drop in on Tomb Number 55. You'll be on your own because the tour groups don't bother with it. Notations inside the tomb suggest it was originally built for Akhenaten's mother, but she was not the person found inside the coffin. The identifying details have been deliberately removed from the coffin lid—which is consistent with the treatment given to anything associated with Akhenaten. Recent testing has shown remarkable similarities in blood and physiology between the corpse in that coffin and the corpse of Tutankhamun—a similarity that could almost be fatherly. Research is continuing. When the break-through comes, you may enjoy being able to say that you once stood in the tomb of the man who invented God.

23 · WATER, EVERYWHERE

It was a chilly New Year's Eve in Venice. I was caught in a nightmare, but it wasn't mine. The nightmare belonged to the double-bass player of the Venetian Chamber Orchestra. I was just an observer, powerless to help him.

I had gone to see a performance of *The Four Seasons* in Antonio Vivaldi's own church—Santa Maria della Pieta on the Riva degli Schiavone, just along the Grand Canal from Piazza San Marco. Although I was sick of hearing *The Four Seasons* as background music in Italian restaurants all over the world, I was curious about the man they called The Red Priest (hair colour, not politics), who never said Mass because of weak lungs, who was driven out of his hometown because of an affair with a soprano, who died a pauper in Vienna, and whose passionate creations were ignored until well into the 20th century.

I like to think of Vivaldi as the musical equivalent of Vincent van Gogh, and *The Four Seasons* as his *Sunflowers* (see Chapter 1). So I was delighted to read on a wall as I arrived in Venice an advertisement for a performance of *The Four Seasons* by the local chamber orchestra, which is apparently a hallowed Venetian tradition on New Year's Eve. This was my chance to have the familiar melodies refreshed by the creaking of the wood and the squeaking of the strings—just as they would have sounded when played in the church by the orchestra of the girls' orphanage where Vivaldi composed and taught music between 1703 and 1740.

Typically for Italy, far too many tickets had been sold to the event, and once all the pews were filled, the late arrivals had to sit on folding chairs around the altar, leaving a small circular space where the instruments and music stands had been set up for the seven musicians. As we milled about, a man took a short cut from one side of the altar to the other, and knocked over one of the music stands. The sheets of music spilled out everywhere. He bent over, hurriedly bundled them up and shoved them back into the folder. Then he righted the stand and shamefacedly disappeared into the crowd. I was beginning to wonder how I might warn the musicians when they walked out from behind the altar and took their seats.

Briskly they opened their folders and the lead violinist prepared to launch into 'Spring'. My eyes were on the double-bass player. Novelists often write about characters who 'go white in the face', but I had never seen it until that night. He began frantically to shuffle through the music sheets, and I could almost read his mind: 'How could this happen? I set this up half an hour ago with the pages in order. Now they're all over the place. Is someone trying to ruin my life? Which one of them was it? I'll kill the bastard. Don't start yet, oh please don't start yet'.

He must have concluded that reordering the pages was hopeless, because he picked up his double-bass and his chair and moved over to sit behind the cello player, reading the sheet music over the cellist's shoulder until the end of the first half.

Perhaps the performance suffered, but I couldn't tell. Sitting two metres away from the musicians, I was swamped in sound. When I closed my eyes, I pictured Vivaldi as the violinist, surrounded by young women sawing at their strings and gazing at him adoringly. When I opened my eyes I was looking up at a ceiling fresco painted by Tiepolo around 1755. It's called *The Triumph of Faith*.

You may be wondering what this has to do with water, which is ostensibly the theme of this chapter. I must admit that I've been dying to tell that story ever since it happened, and a chapter about water gives me an excuse. Venice, after all, is defined by its water. Without it, Vivaldi wouldn't have been there, and neither would I.

I'd argue that a body of water is essential for a city to have any claims to greatness. Think about the legendary places of the world. Hong Kong, San Francisco, New York, Rio, Sydney and Barcelona have their harbours. Toronto, Chicago, Lucerne and Kampala have their lakes. Paris has the Seine, London has the Thames, Florence has the Arno, New Orleans the Mississippi, and Prague the Vltava. Amsterdam invented itself by building canals.

Recognising the importance of rivers, Vienna pretends to have the Danube, but really what you're looking at in the middle of town is a rather dull canal. (The real Donau, which is not blue but green and muddy, is on the outskirts of Vienna near Mexicoplatz, and if you are truly masochistic you can go onto an artificial island in the middle of the river and watch the Viennese bicycling in the nude). The cities which have a more legitimate claim to the Danube are Bratislava and Budapest, but the Viennese PR machine and Johann Strauss got there first. And a canal is better than nothing.

Now think about the blandest big cities of the world—the likes of Los Angeles, Milan, Tel Aviv, Beijing, Pretoria and Santiago—and you realise that while they may sometimes be near the coast, or have trickles in their suburbs, they are not refreshed and inspired and defined by a river or harbour or lake. Waterless cities are pushing uphill to persuade interesting people to keep living in them or to visit them. Bologna managed the trick by focusing on indoor pleasures. Madrid developed a vibrant street life, especially at night, that distracts attention from its dusty dryness. They are the only exceptions I can think of to my principle.

So this chapter is about some of the places in the world that are made essential by their water. Egypt is a model of this phenomenon. More than 80 percent of it is uninhabitable. Its cities only exist because of the Nile, an assemblage of water that is wonderful for looking at and for floating on, but which should not be touched, swum in or swallowed, unless you are seeking to contract a disorder called bilharzia and have a parasite enter your skin and do terrible things to your liver, bladder, lungs and nervous system.

This should not deter you, however, from going for a glide on a *felucca*, a wide wooden boat with a single sail which is the most ancient mode of commercial transportation still operating in the world. Some people get over-enthusiastic and hire a felucca between Luxor and Aswan, a three-day journey that can get pretty uncomfortable as you lie on the deck in your sleeping bag and take your chances with the food the boatman provides. I found that an hour drifting on a felucca in the middle of Cairo was enough to calm nerves jangled by the noise, dirt and crowds of the city. It proved that humans can live anywhere as long as there is water on which to escape. I resisted the temptation to trail my hand in the river.

The best place to reflect on the Nile's 10,000 year history as the amniotic fluid of human civilisation is from the corniche. Every Egyptian city has one. In theory, a corniche is an elegant promenade of gardens, shops and grand hotels along a river bank. In practice, only the corniche at Aswan is anything like that. Luxor's corniche is in a permanent state of about-to-be-repaired, with piles of paving stones tripping you every few metres. And most of Cairo's corniche is too close to traffic for comfortable strolling. However, you should walk to the southern end of the corniche that runs along Roda Island (where the posh people live, in the middle of the river). There you'll reach a strange structure called the Nilometer, built in the 9th century AD to measure the height of the river and therefore its likely effect on the harvest. You need to knock on the door of the caretaker's cottage and ask for the key. Then you can descend the stairs and examine the column that used to tell the Egyptians whether they would feast or starve for the following year. The Nilometer is useless now, because the unpredictability of the water level has been smoothed out by the construction of the Aswan Dam. The Egyptians decided to control their water, instead of being ruled by it.

Almost as important as water for a great city is a bridge, which provides a frame to display the river or harbour. Bridges let you imbibe the tranquillity of the water without needing to board a boat; they offer a way to stand back and evaluate the city. I can never understand why people commit suicide from bridges, since I find them to be antidotes to depression. The ancient Romans obviously thought so too. The chief priest of ancient Rome was called the Pontifex Maximus, literally the great bridge-maker, because the city's bridges were symbols of good luck. The word turned into Pontiff, which presumably makes the Pope these days the guardian of the world's bridges, or at least the Catholic ones.

In the movie *Sabrina* (the 1996 version), the gruff businessman Linus Larrabee (Harrison Ford) falls in love with his chauffeur's daughter as she gives this analysis of Paris: 'Along the Seine there's a four-mile walk that goes from the Ile Ste Germaine to the Pont d'Austerlitz. It takes you past all the bridges of Paris—23 of them. And you find the one you love and you go there every day with your coffee and your journal and you listen to the river.' Linus: 'What does it tell you?' Sabrina: 'That's between you and the river.' My bet is that the one Sabrina loved was the Pont des Arts, which is only for walkers.

My favourite bridge is a covered wooden structure that crosses the river Brenta in the town of Bassano del Grappa in northern Italy. I walked onto it at sunset, and the view of town and mountains was unbeatable. I learned later that it was called the Ponte degli Alpini and that it had been designed by Palladio in 1599. Maybe that was why I found it so pretty and peaceful, or maybe it was the fact that I had been sampling the local liqueur during the afternoon. Italy's Alpine troops in World War I adopted Bassano's bridge as their symbol and grappa as their drink. That was the war they won. And I can testify that one of the best brands of grappa happens to be called Da Ponte.

Some towns are known only by their bridges. Certainly that was what kept me in the southern French city of Avignon longer than the time necessary to hire a car and drive on to Arles. And one of the great disappointments of my life was finding that they don't dance on the bridge there. In fact, they never did.

Anyone who has learned French has had to sing the nursery rhyme *Sur le pont d'Avignon, on y danse, on y danse. Sur le pont d'Avignon, on y danse tous en rond.* ('On the bridge of Avignon, one dances there, one dances there. On the bridge of Avignon, one dances there all in a circle.') So my first pilgrimage after I got off the TGV (Train of Great Speed) from Paris was to the bridge of St Benezet. It was built in the 12th century, when angels helped a shepherd boy named Benezet erect it for the glory of the deity, and restored in the 15th century. But it's a sorry sight these days. Half of the arches were washed away in a flood, so it doesn't go anywhere, and local safety officers have erected barriers to stop walkers.

Even in its prime, Benezet's bridge could not have been wide enough for any group of persons to dance in a circle. Further investigation reveals that the original song didn't say *sur le pont* but *sous le pont* ('under the bridge')—a reference to the practice of dancing on an island in the middle of the Rhone. But you can't even do that any more, because the span doesn't reach that far.

Bridge buffs in Avignon can be more than compensated for that disappointment by driving southwards for half an hour and stopping at the Pont du Gard. Now *this* is a bridge, or more accurately a three-decker sandstone aqueduct built by the Romans 2000 years ago and still spanning the Gardon Valley. You can walk across the top of the aqueduct, right through a 275 metre stretch of stone pipe that carried 20,000 cubic metres of water a day on its journey to the city of Nimes. The Romans thought nothing of building a pipeline from a spring in the mountains and getting it to maintain a gentle downward slope for 50 kilometres till it reached the town. Imagine the planning that required, and the engineering. And Napoleon thought nothing of renovating it in the early 19th century.

The Pont du Gard is so impressive that I could understand how some travellers might devote their lives to finding the great aqueducts of the world. I have been content with visiting just one other—the aqueduct through Segovia in Spain, built by the Emperor Trajan in the 2nd century, renovated by Queen Isabella in the 15th, and still part of the city's water supply system until the 1970s. It has two tiers, compared with the Pont du Gard's three, but its slender columns and arches soar over the streets, glowing in the sun in summer and lined with snow in the winter. The Segovia aqueduct is a permanent symbol of the city's glorious antiquity and a useful framework for hanging banners during festivals.

The uplifting nature of the Segovia aqueduct suggests to me a solution for those cities which lack a river, lake or harbour. If you don't have any water for a bridge to cross, build a bridge anyway, and run the water over the land. An aqueduct is an asset to any environment. The only problem may be finding engineers capable of planning and erecting it. Quality standards in the building industry have slipped somewhat since Roman times.

24 · XANADU

Officially, the capital of the State of California is a dusty town called Sacramento. But the capital of the state of mind called California is Xanadu. It is the embodiment of the Californian dream—massive individual wealth unrestrained by taste, discretion or common sense.

Xanadu is also known as Hearst Castle. It was built during the 1920s on the coastline between LA and San Francisco by the newspaper magnate William Randolph Hearst, who usually referred to it as 'the ranch'. His architect called it La Cuesta Encantada ('the enchanted hill'). George Bernard Shaw said it was 'what heaven would be like if God had Hearst's money'. And the state of California calls it a miracle, because Hearst Castle is the only National Historic Landmark that makes a profit (costing around $12 million a year to maintain, and earning $15 million a year from the 30,000 people who visit each week). By donating the ranch to California in

1958, the Hearst family gave their state a nice little earner and their patriarch an immortality he did not deserve.

It was Orson Welles who referred to Hearst Castle as Xanadu in the film *Citizen Kane*. He drew on the poem *Kubla Khan*, written by Samuel Taylor Coleridge after a drug-induced hallucination, which began 'In Xanadu did Kubla Khan a stately pleasure dome decree ... '. When he saw Hearst Castle, Welles was reminded of Coleridge's description: 'So twice five miles of fertile ground/With walls and towers were girdled round ... Through wood and dale the sacred river ran,/Then reached the caverns measureless to man'.

These days you have to book your visit to Xanadu at least a week in advance. It seems that everybody is queuing to compare Hearst's fantasy with their own. Four different 90-minute tours operate simultaneously, because one tour could not begin to show the 150 densely decorated rooms in the main house and the three guest houses, each a palace in its own right, plus the indoor and outdoor Roman baths, the gardens, the zoo, the private cinema, and the vaults stuffed with art treasures that couldn't fit upstairs.

William Randolph Hearst came by his wealth the old-fashioned way—he inherited it. But in true Californian style he quadrupled the millions from his father's silver mines by running 26 newspapers, 15 magazines and 11 radio stations, so that by the mid-1920s he had a personal income of $20 million a year. He tried to buy the presidency of the United States, but he was thwarted by his own erratic personality. He tried to buy critical acclaim for his mistress, an actress named Marion Davies, but he was thwarted by her lack of talent. He tried to become a great publisher, but his newspapers are remembered for their dishonesty, their sensationalism and their sycophantic pursuit of the proprietor's whims.

But Hearst did manage to buy much of the history of Europe and the Middle East. As he travelled, he plundered whole churches, temples, mansions and palaces and shipped the booty back to the town of San Simeon on the west coast of America. Then he ordered his architect, Julia Morgan, to incorporate them in the labyrinth that kept growing on top of the hill behind the town. You could say he was the ultimate obsessive traveller.

As the project got under way in 1921 (when Hearst was 58), Morgan wrote to two antique dealer friends in what we can interpret as an exasperated tone, summarising what Hearst had collected 'from the ends of the earth' for inclusion in his dream home: 'vast quantities of tables, armoires, secretaires, all kinds of cabinets, polychrome church statuary, columns, door frames, carved doors in all stages of repair and disrepair, over-altars, reliquaries, lanterns, iron grille doors, window grilles, votive candlesticks, torches, all kinds of chairs in quantity, six or seven well heads . . . I don't see myself where we are ever going to use half suitably, but I find that the idea is to try things out and if they are not satisfactory, discard them for the next thing that comes along that promises better'.

Having surrounded himself with the physical opulence he required, Hearst set about finding the right company. He would invite his favourites from the worlds of entertainment and politics to stay at the ranch, and treat them lavishly. A 'home movie' shown to modern visitors in the 50-seat cinema suggests that Charlie Chaplin was a frequent guest, along with Winston Churchill, Errol Flynn, Carole Lombard, David Niven and Buster Keaton.

Hearst would serve dinners for 40 on a medieval oak

bench with 18th century silverware, but demonstrate his frugality by using paper serviettes and leaving the mustard and tomato sauce in their bottles. The Roy Rogers band played Hearst's favourite song, *Tumbling Tumbleweed*, from a balcony he had salvaged from a 15th century French abbey. He kept a generous supply of jellybeans in a 16th century ebony and crystal presentation case. The only complaint registered by his guests was that they were sometimes kept awake by the roaring of the pet lions and tigers.

In an obituary which might give some modern media barons pause for reflection, *Time* magazine in 1951 summarised Hearst's life: 'No other press lord ever wielded his power with less sense of responsibility. No other press ever matched the Hearst press for flamboyance, perversity and incitement of mass hysteria. Hearst never believed in anything much, not even Hearst, and his appeal was not to men's minds but to those infantile emotions which he never conquered in himself: arrogance, hatred, frustration, fear'.

It's curious that the obituarist left greed out of the final list—perhaps that is not seen as a negative in the context of California. The obituary also failed to acknowledge Hearst's important contribution to America's mythology. For that, we must look to the official guidebook published by Hearst Castle: 'In 1919 William Randolph Hearst, a mighty newspaper publisher, and Julia Morgan, a prominent architect, began to create a world all its own on a remote hilltop, a world designed to be the supreme expression of that idolised part of our culture, the California dream ... Millions of visitors have already found La Cuesta Encantada to be a potent, indivisible sum of its many parts, a masterwork of lasting vitality, a dream-come-true as enduring as the bedrock that underlies it'. No doubt the author of the guidebook would apply the last line of Coleridge's poem to Hearst: 'For he on honeydew had fed, and drunk the milk of paradise'.

The dream that Xanadu embodies can be summed up in three words: Anything Is Possible. It's the dream that brings to California every year 200,000 new settlers from elsewhere in America and many more illegal immigrants from across the Mexican border. The vital statistics seem to justify their decision. With 30 million citizens, California is the most powerful of America's states. If it were a separate nation it would have the sixth biggest economic output in the world. The per capita income of its residents is higher than that of any nation except a couple of Arab oil kingdoms.

Yet California has trouble being taken seriously. New Yorkers will tell you it's loony-land—'the continent tilts to the left and all the loose bits roll westwards', said Frank Lloyd Wright. Few would argue with the proposition that everything happens first in California, but when Californians say that, they are thinking of the silicon chip, the movie industry and commercial aviation, while east coasters are thinking of hot tubs, crystals and Ronald Reagan. Both are right.

For 100 years California has been the laboratory of ideas for the western world. Growing from a gold rush and with regular infusions of political and social refugees, it developed the perfect mix of a high sense of adventure and no sense of shame. Its readiness to take risks brought it immense wealth and immense influence, but not much respect. Here are 20 big ideas of the 20th century that, for better or worse, came out of California:

1. The anti-Vietnam War movement
2. The Big Bang theory of the universe
3. Biotechnology

4. Celebrity politicians
5. Chardonnay
6. Freeways
7. Gay militancy
8. Hippies
9. Hot tubs (jacuzzis)
10. Jeans
11. Mickey Mouse
12. The movies
13. New age consciousness
14. 'Pacific Rim' cuisine
15. Personal computers
16. Personalised number plates
17. Profitable Olympic Games
18. The silicon chip
19. Skateboards
20. The tax revolt

Kevin Starr, former chief librarian of San Francisco and the author of four books on the history of California, says the state is driven by two powerful obsessions—love of technological innovation and love of nature. 'It's a very Californian assumption that if you have a good idea you can always find someone to take a risk and back you,' he says. 'The high-tech revolution began here in 1928, when Stanford University set aside land for an industrial park and two young Stanford graduates named Hewlett and Packard got together and began to develop ideas.

'Then there's this long tradition of commitment to nature and health—the idea of being released into an endemic garden. This has turned into environmentalism, which provides an encompassing mythology, theology, politics, a way of being. In the 1960s the sexual revolution became a whole way of life. Now environmentalism represents that same kind of liberating release that galvanises the thinking Californians and gives them purpose.'

California now seems to me a model of what Australia will be early next century— a multicoloured collection of immigrants, clinging to the ocean, blessed by climate, getting tough on crime, cynical about politicians, with its Anglo-Saxons discovering they are about to be less than 50 percent of the population, and its middle classes moving to high-security suburban enclaves to escape the dirt and disorder of the cities.

Kevin Starr shared my sense of the similarities. He says California developed as a coastal strip on the edge of a desert, just like eastern Australia. 'In the long run you Australians have still not domesticated the interior of your continent—there's a great big hole there,' he says. 'Psychologically, California is the same. To us the rest of the continent is another country.'

The key difference between Australia and California is in the mechanism for political change. Other countries elect governments which either implement or forget policy promises. Californians elect a government and then bypass it, running their lives by constant referendums, which they call 'ballot initiatives'. Collect enough signatures on a petition and you can put any idea to the voters. If it succeeds, the government is obliged to implement it. In the late 1970s Californians decided they were overgoverned and overtaxed. In two initiatives they voted to reduce their property taxes and to restrict government's ability to collect and spend further tax revenue. That 'tax revolt' spread through America and the theme of 'getting government off our backs' brought Ronald Reagan into the presidency.

The long-term result was a dramatic decline in

California's quality of life. The state that once boasted about its great schools, modern highways, beautiful beaches and humane social safety net now worries about clogged streets, unaffordable housing, gang warfare, homeless beggars, dirty air, the growing gulf between rich and poor, too little water and too much garbage. But imbued with the spirit of Anything Is Possible, Californians think they can solve the problems by radical action.

Robert Bell thinks the answer lies in turning California's psychological separation from the rest of America into reality. He runs an organisation called Citizens for California's Independence, which argues that California should secede and declare itself a nation in its own right. Bell works as an office supplies salesman in Los Angeles, but he devotes all his spare time to collecting signatures for a petition to have the issue put to the voters. 'California cannot be adequately governed by a president and Congress three thousand miles away,' he says. 'I want to put the destiny of California back in the hands of Californians. California can become the leading economic power in the world. It would not rival Japan, it would pass Japan and provide the highest standard of living for its citizens.' How would the rest of the country feel about the nation's economic powerhouse cutting itself off? 'The United States would see California as a formidable foe and would choose not to fight,' says Bell confidently.

Running parallel with Bell's campaign for secession is a campaign to split California into three states. The visionary behind this project is Stan Statham, a Republican member of the State Assembly. He says a population of 30 million is simply unmanageable by one central government, particularly when there is such social and economic diversity. He started by campaigning to have California divided into two states—one coastal and one inland—but was quickly brought into line when voters on the north coast rejected the idea in a referendum. They weren't opposed to smaller political units. They just did not want to be part of a state that included Los Angeles. 'I made a mistake in not recognising how San Franciscans feel about Los Angeles,' Statham said. Now he talks of a division into Northern California (population 2.5 million) Central California (10 million) and Southern California (18 million). Even if his proposal does not pass, it provides a useful way for the visitor to comprehend the vastness of the place. Here's how I would differentiate the three Californias:

1. **Northern.** *Environment:* fog and redwood forests. *Industries:* computers and wine. *Capital:* San Francisco. *Foodstyle:* Italian adventurous. *Most famous local resident:* Robin Williams. *Recommended visiting time:* one week.

2. **Southern.** *Environment:* beaches, palm trees and pollution. *Industries:* movies and television. *Capital:* Los Angeles (do not bother with San Diego). *Foodstyle:* Nouvelle Japanese-Mexican-French. *Most famous local resident:* Kevin Costner. *Recommended visiting time:* five days if you hire a car; three weeks if you don't.

3. **Central.** *Environment:* deserts and canyons. *Industry:* farming. *Capital:* Fresno. *Foodstyle:* spare ribs. *Most famous local resident:* Roy Rogers. *Recommended visiting time:* well, that would depend on whether you share my fascination with weird small museums, because Central California abounds with them.

You can easily spend a week among such splendours as the Roy Rogers Cowboy Museum in Victorville, the Barbie Doll Hall of Fame in Palo Alto, the Winchester

Mystery House in San Jose, The Banana Museum in Altadena, the Thermometer Museum in Sacramento and the Western Ski Museum in Soda Springs.

If your time is limited, then there is one small museum which transcends all the others. It is called Exotic World, and, like Hearst Castle, it is a triumphant celebration of individualism. It's in the desert about 200 kilometres east of Los Angeles, on the outskirts of a village of 4000 souls called Helendale. In a large white-washed bungalow a venerable lady named Dixie Evans runs Exotic World as a monument to a lost art form and as a shrine to one of America's greatest practitioners of the art, Jenny Lee, known to her fans as The Bazoom Girl, or Miss 44 And Plenty More.

In the 1950s Jenny Lee created the world's first trade union for striptease artists, The Exotic Dancers League of America, and fought many battles against exploitation by club managers. When she retired, she founded Exotic World in a couple of rooms of her house, and when she died (of breast cancer, I'm afraid), one of her proteges, Dixie Evans, inherited her collection of g-strings, tassels, programmes, posters and gifts from adoring fans, as well as Jayne Mansfield's original heart-shaped couch.

Dixie Evans dusts the displays and polishes the urn containing the ashes of Jenny Lee (engraved 'In Loving Memory Virginia Lee Arroya 1928-1990') but she really comes to life when a visitor arrives at the museum. She tells you the history of burlesque ('It's an American art, like baseball') and presents you with an autographed photograph of Jenny Lee inscribed 'Bust Wishes'. She confides that she herself was born in the same year as Marilyn Monroe, and for many years did a strip act in which she pretended to *be* Marilyn Monroe. It occurred to me that if Monroe had lived, she might well, at the age of 69, be sitting alone in some sort of museum in the desert of Central California, waiting for her one visitor a day and still thinking that Anything Is Possible.

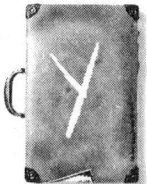

25 · YQUEM, FRANCE

Here's the legend: once upon a time a winemaker in southwestern France was called away from his vineyard to fight in a war. By the time he had returned, the normal picking time had passed and his grapes were mouldy and shrivelled on the vines. He should have thrown them away and waited till next year, but he was desperate, so he told his workers to pick them anyway and do their best to make something drinkable. Pessimistically he tried the result, and discovered a miracle—a luscious honey nectar that tasted even better when sipped with a fruity dessert, or creamy cheeses, or liver, or strong fish. That wine came to be known as Chateau d'Yquem (pronounced shatto deekem). It is now regarded (by the French, anyway) as the greatest white wine in the world. Certainly it's the most expensive.

That tale of victory snatched from the mouth of defeat grew up because the real origins of Yquem are obscure. Traditionally the disease that creates the intense flavour—botrytis cinerea, which the French now call 'noble rot'—was a plague that winemakers struggled to avoid. The plague flourished in the autumn mists of a land called Sauternes. The estate originally owned by the Yquem family, being at the highest point in the district, was most vulnerable to it. Nowadays the winemakers at Yquem are as desperate to attract the disease as their ancestors were to avoid it. In the years when the botrytis does not shrivel the grapes enough to suit their standards, they don't produce Yquem at all. They use the grapes to make a plain old white just called 'Y' (which is pronounced eegrec). That last happened in 1992.

I decided to make a pilgrimage to the source of Yquem after I sampled it at $23 a glass in the Union Square Cafe in New York back in 1988. The experience was so exquisite I wanted to know how the effect was achieved, and how any wine could justify such a price. So I planned a journey around it, and a year later a friend and I flew to Paris, took the train to Bordeaux, hired a car and drove to Sauternes, arriving about 1pm.

Sauternes proved to be a windy village with one church, one garage, and a couple of rows of grey houses. There was nobody in sight as we got out of the car, but we heard the faint sound of laughter from a side street. It seemed logical to follow it, and we reached a wooden building with red gingham curtains that was clearly a cafe. We pushed open the door to discover that all life was here. It was filled with shouting people and smoke from a fire of vine branches, over which hung a row of spitting lamb chops. There was no menu—everyone had vegetable soup, lamb chops and apple tart. And no wine list—everyone had glasses of different sauternes with each course.

The locals filled us with information about the most

interesting way to walk to Chateau d'Yquem. Around 3 p.m. we set off unsteadily, past vineyards that are almost as legendary as Yquem but not as well placed for the breezes that bring the botrytis in the autumn, until finally we trespassed onto the edge of the Yquem estate. Since every vineyard in Bordeaux is called a chateau, even if the only structure on the property is a tin shed, we were somewhat surprised to find that there is a genuine castle at Yquem—a 13th century fortress of light brown sandstone with witch hat towers on a roof made of terracotta tiles.

We stood watching the activities in the vineyard for an hour. Two images stay in my mind: horses pulling single-bladed ploughs to turn the soil between the rows of grapes, because mechanical equipment might be too brutal; and workers wandering around inspecting individual bunches of grapes and snipping off leaves with scissors so that the sun would strike each grape appropriately. I wanted to know more.

It appears that the Yquem estate was already making sweet wine at the time that a Miss Yquem married a Mr Lur-Saluces (pronounced loor salloos) in 1785. It was the Lur-Saluces family who introduced it to the world. The first famous customer was an American named Thomas Jefferson, who was sent as ambassador to France by the brand new US Government. In 1788 he toured the wine areas seeking information on how to set up an industry in the US. He decided that the most esteemed wines came from the area called Sauternes, and wrote in his journal: 'The best crop belongs to M. Diquem at Bordeaux, or to M. de Salus his son-in-law.' (Does this sound like someone who had difficulty deciphering his notes after a pleasant day's sampling?) Back in Philadelphia in 1790, Jefferson wrote to the Lur-Saluces: 'The white wine of Sauternes, of your growth, was so well received by the

Americans who tasted it that I do not doubt it will conform generally to the taste of my compatriots. Now that I am established here I have persuaded our President, General Washington, to try a sample. He asks for thirty dozen, sir, and I ask you for ten dozen for myself'.

Jefferson became President of the United States in 1801, which may have made him too busy to finish all ten dozen bottles, because recently the present owner of the Yquem vineyard, Alexandre de Lur-Saluces, was able to buy at auction a bottle of the 1774 vintage with Thomas Jefferson's name written on it. It will never be opened, so there's no way of knowing if the wine still tastes good. Lur-Saluces says the oldest Yquem he has tasted was the 1847 vintage, and that is holding up pretty well.

So why is Yquem so expensive? Because of the way it is made. Lur-Saluces says it is a mixture of about 80 percent semillon grapes and 20 percent sauvignon grapes, but the proportions vary each year as the wine is 'tuned till its note is perfection'. All the grapes from one vine go to produce just one glass of wine (the usual ratio in Bordeaux is a bottle per vine). The only fertiliser used on the vines comes from 30 contented cows who are kept on the nearby Chateau de Fargues estate, which Lur-Saluces also owns. In September the vineyard workers go around snipping off leaves to ensure the sunshine reaches the grapes. Then in October the picking begins. About 120 pickers walk through the vines day after day, examining every bunch and choosing only those grapes which are shrunken and covered with mould. Some days they find no fruit worth picking. The process can take eight weeks. Says Lur-Saluces: 'Yquem costs so much because I pay people to do nothing!'

After fermentation, the wine is stored in new oak barrels for three and a half years. The barrels are only used once. In a good year the total production from a vineyard that covers 173 hectares is 95,000 bottles. The cheapest vintage you can find at the moment is the 1989—at around $600 a bottle—and anything earlier is likely to top the $1000 mark, which makes my glass at the Union Square Cafe seem cheap. The most admired post-war vintage was 1967, and a bottle of that would be a bargain at $5000. Alexandre de Lur-Saluces observes: 'People who don't understand what is done at Yquem criticise the price. When they understand, they can't believe we don't receive government grants'.

It's an interesting philosophical question whether the sensual experience you could gain from a glass of wine could ever be worth $1000. I'm inclined to think it could not. Lur-Saluces says what he does is 'economically stupid, but gastronomically wise'. I'll be lucky if I drink a glass of Chateau d'Yquem twice more in my lifetime, but I'm pleased to be living in a world where perfectionism is still possible.

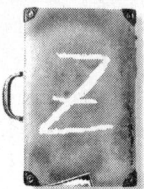

26 · ZURICH, SWITZERLAND

I'm sitting at the bar of James Joyce Pub, just off the Bahnhofstrasse in Zurich, drinking a coffee with Max Schafer, a vice president of the Union Bank of Switzerland. Schafer, a round man in his early 50s, is a bit depressed. James Joyce Pub exists as the result of an act of generosity by his bank (Switzerland's biggest), which bought the Victorian bar of Jury's Hotel in Dublin in the late 1970s and shipped it, tile by tile and stool by stool, to the centre of Zurich. It was then reconstructed with meticulous attention to detail, and renamed in honour of one of the city's most illustrious visitors. Even the drink coasters are printed with the warning they bore when the bar was in Dublin: 'Drivers please don't have one for the road and risk your licence. We want to see you more than once a year'.

But somehow, Max Schafer feels, a certain atmosphere has been lost in translation. When he visited pubs in Dublin, they were full of noise and smoke and laughter. James Joyce Pub is quiet. 'In Dublin, you could say hello to someone at the bar, and strike up a conversation,' Schafer says. 'In Zurich, if you said hello to someone at the bar, he would wonder what you wanted from him.' Schafer doesn't like to reflect too much on what that says about the Swiss, or at least about the German-speaking Swiss who predominate in Zurich.

As we drift into the topic of national characteristics, I ask if it is true that every home in Switzerland has a gun in it. 'Oh yes,' says Schafer proudly. 'I have ten guns in my home, because I am a captain in the army.' (Switzerland has no full-time army but all adult males are in the civilian defence force, doing three weeks training a year, and they must have weapons instantly ready in case of a threat to the fatherland.) I tell Schafer that gun control is a big issue in Australia, and wonder if there isn't a risk that some Swiss would use their guns for crime, or go mad and commit mass murder. He looks puzzled. 'A Swiss would never use his army gun for crime,' he says. 'It's the ethic. If you were going to commit a crime, you would get another gun. Except for suicide, of course. People sometimes use their army guns for that.'

Why would anyone want to commit suicide in the most wealthy, beautiful and democratic nation in Europe? After all, the Swiss have achieved what looks like perfection in their political system. Citizens can be called upon to vote as often as eight times a year—for their central government or their canton government or their district council, or in various local and national referendums. Usually less than 40 percent of eligible voters bother to participate—possibly because they are satisfied with the status quo, or possibly because they know it would make little difference if they changed their party allegiance. The central government has been the same coalition of four parties, representing 80 percent of the voters, since 1959. The national government, the 23 canton governments, and the 3061 local councils (yes, 3085 governments for a population of six million!) consult the citizens regularly via referendums, and if the politicians fail to put an issue to the vote, a petition of 50,000 signatures can initiate a referendum anyway.

The Swiss also seem to have managed the most successfully multicultural society in the world. The best joke I was told there went like this—a German, a Frenchman and a Swiss were discussing where babies come from. The German said: 'Everybody knows that the stork brings them.' The Frenchman laughed, and said: 'In France we know that babies come from a man and a woman making love.' They turned to the Swiss and asked what he thought. He said: 'In Switzerland, it varies from canton to canton.'

The Swiss are proud of their linguistic and religious diversity, and work hard to maintain it. The central government heavily subsidises the remote mountainous area in the southeast, inhabited by the speakers of the Romansh language (a bit like Latin), because there's a tendency for the young people to drift to the big population centres in search of work or excitement, and to lose their cultural identity. There are five newspapers published in the Romansh language—a pretty wide choice for a population of 50,000 people.

Nobody seems to mind that the German-speaking Swiss in the north accuse the Italian-speaking Swiss in the south and the French-speaking Swiss in the west of being lazy hedonists, while the French speakers accuse the German speakers of being fat sausage eaters, and the Italian speakers accuse the German speakers of being greedy 'squareheads'. The system could be described as 'snobbery within harmony'.

The apparent perfection of Switzerland is the reason I made its economic capital one of my essential places. Every society wants to be rich, humane and harmonious. The Swiss must have a lot to teach us. And yet, when you ask them, they don't seem to like their perfection much. They engage in a degree of self-criticism which verges on self-abuse. I lost count of the number of conversations which began 'Why do you want to write about us—we're very boring'. They would then point out that Switzerland has problems with AIDS and drug addiction, as if to prove they have something in common with less mature nations after all.

They almost sympathise with the observation of Orson Welles, in a piece of dialogue he wrote for the character of Harry Lime in *The Third Man:* 'In Italy for 30 years under the Borgias they had warfare, terror, murder, bloodshed. They produced Michelangelo, Leonardo da Vinci and the Renaissance. In Switzerland, they had brotherly love, 500 years of democracy and peace. And what did they produce? The cuckoo clock'. More recently, the actor Peter Ustinov, who lives in Switzerland, observed that the Swiss have 'lightened the burden of efficient existence by totally discarding the unnecessary weight of humour and irony'. They even go about their comedy with clockwork precision. But then, says Ustinov: 'Imagination of a kind may be lacking, but with a landscape as unique as that of Switzerland, who needs fantasy?'

The Swiss have a lot in common with the people of Hong Kong (see Chapter 11), in their fascination with money and in the obvious material success of their society. But while Hong Kong celebrates superstition, believing in everything, Switzerland revels in realism, believing in common sense. As I was planning to go in search of the birthplace of William Tell, I received a press release from the National Tourist Office which said: 'Switzerland must be the only country to have a national hero, known the world over, who did not exist'. I don't wish to know that. The British would never destroy my illusions about Robin Hood and King Arthur, and I'll thank the Swiss to leave me with my fantasies about crossbows and apples. They won't, though. The definition of a Swiss is someone who, if forced to park illegally, phones the police and informs on himself.

More precisely, that was given to me as the definition of a Zuricher. According to the southern and western Swiss, Zurich is Boredom Central. Yes, it might be a clean city of low-rise office blocks (surprising in the context of the high-powered transactions that take place there) with gabled houses, cobbled squares and a peaceful lake, but its anal retentiveness borders on neurosis.

And yet Zurich had enough going for it early this century to hold the attention of James Joyce and Vladimir Ilyich Ulyanov (later known as Lenin) during crucial periods of their lives. Lenin, possibly in the absence of anything better to do, drew up the blueprint for a Soviet state at number 14 Spiegelgasse between February 1916 and April 1917, when he left Zurich for Petrograd in a sealed train. His apartment block now has an adult toy shop on the ground floor, which sells red and green busts of Lenin among its clockwork animals.

Joyce wrote the first draft of *Ulysses* at 38 Universitatstrasse between 1915 and 1918. That three-storey house now has a sign outside advertising a clinic for *Wiederherstellungschirurgie*, which I think means plastic surgery. Joyce returned to Zurich in late 1940—once again to escape a war in the rest of Europe—and died there in January 1941. His grave at Fluntern, near the city zoo, features a jaunty life-size metal sculpture of him with his legs crossed.

The world's second-greatest psychoanalyst, Carl Jung, spent all his working life from 1900 in Zurich (when he wasn't in Vienna arguing with the world's greatest psychoanalyst). Despite remarking that Zurich related to the world 'not through intellect but through commerce', Jung managed to come up with the theory of archetypes and the role of mythology in the human unconscious by analysing the Swiss, which may contradict Peter Ustinov's view that they suffer a deficiency of imagination.

Zurich was also the birthplace of the Dada movement, which started in 1916 as a reaction against complacency in the arts, and ultimately inspired surrealism, cubism, theatre of the absurd, beatnik poetry and just about every other 'revolutionary' artistic expression this century. Dada began in a venue called the Cabaret Voltaire (just down the road from Lenin's flat, at 1 Spiegelgasse) where painters, poets, dancers and what nowadays we would call stand-up comedians displayed their work. Dada was apparently a nickname for one of the singers in the cabaret but the word came to symbolise 'anti-art'— an attack on bourgeois ideas of beauty which the Dadaists thought were irrelevant in a time of industrialisation and militarism. The cabaret closed after six months but the idea spread throughout Europe and America.

The nearest Switzerland comes these days to the outrageousness of Dadaism is La Musee de l'Art Brut in Lausanne. The work it displays is designed to prove that the fine line between art and madness is no line at all. The Museum of Outsider Art (a loose translation) scours Europe for the work of what its curator, Michel Thevoz, calls 'people who have not been culturally indoctrinated or socially conditioned—recluses, maladjusted persons, psychiatric hospital patients, inmates of prisons, all kinds of dwellers of the fringes of society'. The collection, he says, owes nothing to tradition or fashion. 'The works are evidence of a power of invention which all men and women possibly possess but which has been stifled in most by educational training and social constraints,' says Thevoz. 'That is why these works at once convey a feeling of alienation and strange familiarity.'

The museum's interior looks like an antique shop on LSD. Apart from the paintings in screaming colour, there are life-size rag dolls, cork carvings, ceramic masks, landscapes of broken plates and bottles, totem poles, pastry sculptures decorated with jujubes, and wooden machines apparently designed to extract confessions from creatures with five legs and three heads.

Next to each display is a biography of the artist, in French and English. We learn that Clement Fraisse was incarcerated in 1925 for setting fire to his family's house with a packet of banknotes. He began carving images into the wooden walls of his cell with a broken spoon. When the spoon was confiscated, he broke off the handle of his chamber pot and carved the walls with that. The walls have been installed in the museum, and Fraisse's intricate panels look like reliefs from gothic churches—plants, figures, animals and arcane symbols.

Guillaume Pujole suffered from 'suicidal melancholy alternating with notions that he was persecuted by his wife and the lover he supposed she had'. In 1926 he was confined in the psychiatric hospital in Toulouse, France, and began a series of nightmarish coloured pencil drawings that place him somewhere between Picasso and Dali, although he never saw the work of either artist.

Augustin Lesage was a coalminer, until one day in 1911 he heard voices telling him to leave the coalface and start painting. His first picture took two years, and he kept producing huge, incredibly detailed canvases under the direction of his spirit guides until his death in 1954.

Adolf Wolfli had to be permanently confined in a mental hospital in 1895 because of his 'abnormal inclination for little girls'. During 20 years alone in a cell, he composed elaborate musical scores, decorating them with paintings. No-one has ever been able to understand the music but the paintings, to a modern eye, are magnificent.

The founder of the collection, the French painter Jean Dubuffet, donated his 5000 items to the city of Lausanne in 1971, and they were put in one wing of a building called the Chateau de Beaulieu. Since then Dubuffet's successors have accumulated another 5000 challenges to the conventions of what is collectible. Dubuffet wanted to explore art which grew directly from the imagination, uninhibited by training and theory. 'These works may often be rudimentary,' he said, 'but they are charged, perhaps more strongly than the works of celebrated artists, with everything that can be asked of a work of art: burning mental tension, uncurbed invention, an ecstasy of intoxication, complete liberty. Mad? Of course. Can you conceive of an art which is not mad?' The Dadaists would have been delighted, and Orson Welles would have been surprised, to find such a collection in Switzerland.

Of course, the Musee de l'Art Brut is in French-speaking Lausanne. In Zurich, they have instead mastered the art of making money. Which was why I was talking to a vice president of Switzerland's biggest bank. I asked Schafer whether the Swiss felt any guilt about the way they've grown rich by looking after the ill-gotten gains of the world's criminals. 'You are talking about capital flight to Switzerland?' he asked. I said yes. 'In the Swiss public that is often a problem that is discussed. But we have a new law which makes money laundering a criminal offence. Under this law it's very hard to launder money through Swiss accounts. Any money coming to Switzerland nowadays is probably whiter than white when it arrives.'

Schafer says Swiss bankers have an undeserved reputation for amorality. The concept of secret numbered accounts arose in the 1930s when the bankers were trying to protect their Jewish customers from investigation by the German Government. The Swiss Government passed a law that any bank employee who revealed information about a customer would be liable to fines and jail terms. 'After the war there were only two currencies that were readily convertible, the US dollar and the Swiss franc,' said Schafer. 'So it made sense if you were in Europe to open a Swiss franc account. Historically, who was in a position to deposit money in Switzerland? It was the rich or the one who had success in his professional career. So at the beginning of the 50s, to have a Swiss account was a reference. Nowadays anyone can open a Swiss franc account, but for some people there is still a kind of snobbery about it, like saying "I have a Mercedes".'

He disputes the notion that much of the foreign money in Swiss banks was deposited by drug dealers and third (or second) world dictators ripping off their own countries. 'We don't need criminal money because that is negligible compared with the honest money,' says Schafer. 'Whenever somebody dies who has a political record you hear a rumour that he had a huge amount in a Swiss bank. It normally starts with a couple of billion, goes down to millions, and then it turns out he hadn't an account. That was, for example, the case of Ceaucescu of Romania. In fact, if a head of state or a well-established politician would like to open an account with us, it needs the approval of general management. It's quite easy to judge on the amounts of money you will deposit whether it's your personal belonging or whether it is state money you want to transfer.'

Strictly speaking, no account is secret any more, since all depositors must identify themselves to bank employees when they first apply. 'We don't open an account, let's say, for Mickey Mouse,' says Schafer, chuckling. (In some banks in Vienna, by contrast, you can open an account without ever giving your name, and use it for as long as you can remember the number.)

These days Swiss bank employees are allowed to give information to police if there is suspicion of drug connections, and Swiss courts can order them to hand over account details if the client has been convicted of a serious crime in another country (although tax avoidance does not, in the Swiss view, constitute a serious crime). Add to all this the fact that the interest rate on savings is pretty low and you'd have to wonder why foreigners in 1996 have made deposits totalling $150 billion in the Union Bank. Schafer says the answer lies in 'the Swiss political stability over the last 100 or 150 years and also the economic stability of the currency'.

In 20 years, the rest of Europe may have collapsed, the dollar may be worth a tenth of its current value, but your Swiss francs will still be as beautiful as the Swiss mountains. It comes back to that clockwork predictability that so infuriated the Dadaists. It's perfect, but the price of perfection is a lifeless pub.

AFTERWORD

This book would not have been possible without many other books to show me the way. Here are some reading suggestions if you should want to venture deeper into the ideas and the environments I discussed . . .

The world's best guidebooks, in my opinion, are produced by Cadogan. They manage to be both informative and cheeky, and they're not afraid to explode myths spread by national tourist offices. I particularly enjoyed the Cadogan guide to Prague (by Sadakat Kadri), and the guides to Spain, Italy and the south of France (all by Dana Facaros and Michael Pauls, whose life I envy).

In Britain and Europe, no scholarly traveller can be without the green Michelin guides, which are at times hilariously solemn but always full of details that might just be useful, such as the heights of cathedrals and the depths of wells. Other European assistance came from *The New Italians* by Charles Richards (Penguin); *Blue Guide Umbria* by Alta Macadam (Black/Norton); *The Food of Italy* and *The Food of France*, both by Waverley Root (Vintage); *The Jews of Spain* by Jane S. Gerber (The Free Press/Macmillan); *The Kingdom by the Sea* by Paul Theroux (Hamish Hamilton); *Notes from a Small Island* by Bill Bryson (Doubleday); *The Viennese: Splendor, Twilight and Exile* by Paul Hofmann (Anchor Press Doubleday); and *Hydra* by Catherine Vanderpool (Lycabettus Press).

Michael Haag's *Guide to Egypt* is fascinating and practical (published by his own company Travelaid, PO Box 369, London NW3 4ER, England). For Hong Kong, I recommend the Fodor Guide and *The Book of Chinese Beliefs* by Frena Bloomfield (Arrow Books). For the United States, I was influenced by *The Heart of the World* by Nik Cohn (Vintage); *The Sky's the Limit: A Century of Chicago Skyscrapers* edited by Pauline A. Saliga (Rizzoli); *Chicago's Famous Buildings* edited by Franz Schulze and Kevin Harrington (The University of Chicago Press); and *The Ultimate Hollywood Tour Book* by William A. Gordon (North Ridge Press). And for Ritzonia, my favorite guide was *Grand Hotel*, designed and produced by Marc Walter (J. M. Dent and Sons). I must also thank the managements of the Ritz, Paris, the Peninsula, Hong Kong, and the Beau-Rivage, Lausanne, for the access they allowed me to their staff and their archives.

To understand the heroes in this book, I read these biographies: *Van Gogh: Letters from Provence*, selected by Martin Bailey (Clarkson Potter); *Van Gogh: A Life* by Philip Callow (Allison and Busby); *Frank Lloyd Wright, Architect: An Illustrated Biography*, by Alexander O. Boulton (Rizzoli); *Frank Lloyd Wright: A Biography* by Meryle Secrest (Chatto and Windus); *Freud: A Life for Our Time* by Peter Gay (Papermac); *The Diary of Sigmund Freud 1929–1939* (The Hogarth Press); *The Complete Tutankhamun* by Nicholas Reeves (Thames and Hudson); and *Hearst Castle: The*

Story of William Randolph Hearst and San Simeon by Taylor Coffman (Sequoia).

Other stimulating notions emerged from *The Tall Building Artistically Reconsidered* by Ada Louise Huxtable (Pantheon); *The Writer's Journey* by Christopher Vogler (Boxtree); *The Intelligent Tourist* by Donald Horne (Margaret Gee Publishing); *The Story of Wine* by Hugh Johnson; *The Innocents Abroad* by Mark Twain (Signet Classic); and *A Little Knowledge* by Michael Macrone (Pavilion).

My final thanks must go to Lisa Highton, who encouraged me to start this book; to Nikki Christer, who forced me to finish it; and to Kirsten Tilgals, whose editing skills saved me from many embarrassments. If they stick around, I might manage volume two.

INDEX

ch'i, 122
Chanel, Coco, 88, 183, 184
Chapel Bridge, Lucerne, 129
Chaplin, Charlie, 135, 159, 184, 226
Charles Bridge, Prague, 165, 166
Charles IV, Emperor, 162
Chesil Beach, Dorset, 46
Christians, viii, x, 112–118, 194–197
Citizen Kane, 225
Claus, Vaclav, 168, 162
Cloud's Hill, Dorset, 47, 48
Cobb, the, Dorset, 42
coffee, 68–69
Columbus, Christopher, 196
communism, ix, 12–14, 16–20, 34,
    163–169, 186, 201
Confucianism, 126
Copernicus, Nicolas, x, 14, 77
Corleone, Sicily, 191
Costner, Kevin, 93, 98, 100, 232
Crusades, the, 116
Czechoslovakia, 18, 161, 166–169
Dadaism, 245, 249
Danube, the, 218, 219
darshana, viii
Darwin, Charles, ix, x, 34–37, 77
Das Kapital, 33, 34
David, King, 112–114
Decameron, 12
Defenestration, 161–169
dim sum, 51–55
Disney studios, LA, 96
Dome of the Rock, Jerusalem, 115
Dorchester, England, 38, 207, 208
Dorset, England, 37–48
Down House, England, 34, 35
Dubcek, Alexander, 18, 19
Dubuffet, Jean, 247
Dylan, Bob, 80, 99
Eco, Umberto, 15
Edward VII, King, 175, 180, 182
Einstein, Albert, ix, x, 77, 118
English, the, 37, 48
Erakor, Vanuatu, 107–111
Escoffier, Auguste, 129, 180–182
ET, 92, 93
Etna, Mount, Sicily, 190
Evans, Dixie, 233
evolution, x, 34, 35

felucca, 219
Ferdinand and Isabella of Spain, 196
Flatiron building, New York, 27, 203
Florence, Italy, 50, 187, 188
fondue, 55, 99,
Ford, Harrison, 93, 221
Form ever follows function, 28
Four Seasons, the, 216, 217
Four Weddings and a Funeral, 92, 97
Fowles, John, xi, 42
Fragonard perfumery, Grasse, 86, 87
Francis, Saint, 155
Freud, Sigmund, viii–x, 74–81, 84,
    175, 209, 251
fung shui, x, 120–125
Galileo, x, 14
geometry, x, 192
George III, King, 38, 47
Gere, Richard, 90, 99
Get Shorty, 98, 101
ghettos, 60, 198
gods: Allah, 116; Amun Ra, 211, 212;
    Aten, 209; Hathor, 214; Khonsu,
    211; Kwan Tai, 126; Mut, 211; Tin
    Hau, 126; Wong Tai Sin, 126;
    Yahweh, 34, 113, 114, 209.
Gotthard pass, Switzerland, 131
Grand Marnier, 181
Grant, Hugh, 92, 100
Greene, Graham, 135
Griffin, Walter Burley, 25
Groucho Club, London, 34
Gubbio, Italy, 155, 156
Hall, Annie, 101
Hall, James, xi, 141
Hapsburg Empire, 75, 76, 167
Hardy, Thomas, 37, 38
Havel, Vaclav, xi, 67, 161, 162,
    164–168
Hearst Castle, California, 224–228
Hearst, William Randolph, xi,
    224–228, 251
hedonism, 13
Hemingway, Ernest, 184
Hercules, 41, 191
Hiassen, Carl, ix, 139–140
Hitler, Adolf, ix, 71, 74–78, 84
Hoffman, Dustin, 95, 98, 99
Holland, 2, 198, 218